WHAT IF...
WE BUILT OUR OWN
SCOUT HALL?

MIKE PHILLIPSON

© 2016 Mike Phillipson

Published by Datacomms Publishing, an imprint of Datacomms (UK) Limited
www.datacomms.org.uk

ISBN 978-1-5262-0346-5

Printed by Catford Print Centre

Front cover and title page artwork credited to James Powell
Rear cover photograph credited to Andy Shennan Photographer

CONTENTS

INTRODUCTION 1

1 – GETTING STARTED 5

    Getting a suitable lease...7

    Convincing ourselves 10

    Convincing our members 11

    The feasibility study... 12

    Estimated build costs 13

    Availability of external funding.. 14

    Internal fund-raising.. 16

    Estimated running costs 17

    Planning consent... 18

    Reigate District Scouts 18

    Network Rail... 19

    Other consultations 19

    Would the Group survive the project?.. 20

    Green for Go.. 22

    In conclusion, what did we learn?.. 23

2 - PLANNING TO RAISE THE MONEY 26

3 – PUTTING THE FUN IN FUNDRAISING 30

    Explorers' hike from Brownsea Island.. 31

    Bag packing.. 33

    Plant sale... 36

    Parish and Group Socials 37

    Raffles (including a prize draw) 40

    Christmas Card Post Service.. 42

A Miscellany of Fairs..43

Race Nights...45

Teas and coffees (and cakes and marmalade and bacon sarnies)..............47

Section-specific fund-raising...48

Santa Walks..49

Carol-singing..51

Friends of the 17th...52

Children's Disco..53

Scavenging materials...53

Flooring..54

Industrial racking 55

Yet more industrial racking (and yet more flooring)..................56

Hoardings...56

Office furniture 57

Lighting..57

Paint...57

Mahogany...57

An old sink..58

Skip-raiding (and reverse skip-raiding) 58

House-clearance..59

Tuck Shop...61

Christmas Craft Morning...61

Crowd-funding..62

Cookie Challenge 63

Donations...63

Mile of Pennies...64

Ideas which fell by the wayside..67

In conclusion, what did we learn?..72

4 – OUR APPROACH TO THE ART OF GRANT APPLICATION 83

Step 1) Find the funders 83

The organization's website 85

The phone call 85

The unsolicited letter (or email) of introduction 87

Our other hunting grounds 88

Similar projects 89

Local or known benefactors 89

Local media 90

Local Government 90

Supporting organizations 91

Well-publicized sources 92

On our doorstep 93

Step 2) Ask them nicely for money 93

Supporting information 94

Making the application 96

Step 3) Expect the cheque, naturally by return mail 99

Step 4) Write them a letter of thanks 101

Step 5) Try and avoid asking them again 102

Step 6) Communicate progress 103

In conclusion, what did we learn? 105

5 – GETTING IT BUILT 110

The legal niceties 110

The design process 112

Nipping off the corner 114

Toilets 115

Waste tank 116

Security 117

Audio-visual facilities 118

Staircase and balustrade 119

Kitchen 119

The fire escape 120

Managing the budget 121

A DIY build 123

What we could not do ourselves 124

What we could do ourselves 126

Stud walls 127

Laying the oak flooring 128

Insulating ceilings and floors 129

Painting 130

The opening ceremony 132

Finishing off and the snagging list 135

In conclusion, what did we learn? 137

Postscript 143

Bibliography 145

Acknowledgements

When, in late 2011, we had this crazy idea to solve 17th Reigate Scout Group's accommodation issue by building our own Scout Hall, little did we realize just how all-consuming the project would become for a great many people over the following four years. Lobbying, negotiating, planning, supervising, managing, and large parts of constructing required thousands of hours of time donated by our amazing team of volunteers. Most of these also had full-time jobs and were juggling involvement in the project with their family, home, and work lives. To name individuals wouldn't be right as so many contributed at different times and in different ways. But you all know who you are and how much you put into the project. 17th Reigate Scout Group and future generations of its young people, as well as the local community, shall forever be grateful and remain in your debt.

An especially big "thank you" goes to our respective ever-patient other halves. These unsung heroes and heroines generally didn't get much choice in helping out, whether physically or by tolerating their husbands/wives disappearing to play at being builders on the site "only for half an hour or so". Without your support and forbearance then achieving what we set out to do would have been so much more difficult.

My thanks to Tony, John, David, Fr. Chris, my wife, my sisters, and my mum for reviewing my first foray into publishing, pointing out in the nicest possible way the omissions and errors, and turning a fairly rough manuscript into an accurate reflection of what we did and how we did it.

Mike Phillipson
Group Scout Leader
17th Reigate (St. Joseph's) Scout Group

INTRODUCTION

"What if" are powerful words with which to begin a sentence. They can lead to great changes. One can imagine an early caveman looking round his cramped space shared with family, friends, and animals and thinking "What if we stacked those rocks over there on top of each other and built our own bigger cave…?" Thus unintentionally heralding the start of the building industry. Or James Watt looking at his kettle boiling away, thinking "What if we could harness the power of the steam coming out …?" And thus drives forward the industrial revolution. Great changes often stem from simple ideas, individuals looking at existing problems and having a light-bulb moment on how to solve them.

17th Reigate Scout Group's own "What if" moment caused change on a less-than-global scale but again demonstrates the power behind the initial thought to create something for the greater good. The back-story is simple and, I suspect, not unfamiliar to many Scout Groups around the country. To explain…

For Scout Groups to succeed, three basic components are needed: enough adult volunteers, enough young people, and somewhere to meet. Being based in a reasonably large town, getting enough young people has never been an issue for 17th Reigate – to date we have around 130 young people and a large waiting-list. We have always been able to attract and retain enough adults to run the Group. The problem we were facing was where to meet.

As one of the few Catholic Scout Groups in Surrey, we have been attached to St. Joseph's Catholic Church in Redhill since the Group's inception 100 years ago. St. Joseph's Church is part of the Parish of the Nativity of the Lord, which in turn falls under the Diocese of Arundel and Brighton. As a benefit from our relationship with St. Joseph's, we had always enjoyed the luxury of being able to use, at no cost to the Group, the church hall – a generously-proportioned building which included (being a Catholic hall), a fully-functioning bar to which we usually and necessarily adjourned after a Scout meeting on a Friday. Times were set to change however; the old hall was dilapidated and had been built in an era where asbestos was popular as a construction material. Refurbishment was long overdue and would be very expensive. The cheapest option would be to demolish the old hall, sell the land for housing development, and use the proceeds to re-build a new Parish Centre elsewhere in the church grounds. This, after many years of debate and procrastination, is what happened. Our Scout Group was in danger of becoming homeless.

Not especially alarmed at this point, we negotiated a sharing deal with a neighbouring Scout Group to whom we shall forever remain indebted as they allowed us to vastly overstay our welcome with forbearance and without complaint even after we burned a large hole in their kitchen worktop (a mishap when our Explorers were making pizzas). Our new temporary home was located in a village a few miles away and was to be found down a long unlit and often very muddy track. No matter, we thought, only for a year or so until the new Parish Centre was built. We eventually vacated after four years.

In the meantime, the plans for the new Parish Centre were published and alarm-bells began to chime in our heads - it was immediately obvious that there would be a few issues. The building was planned to be (and is) high-quality, with posh dangly lights and pristine white walls. It was also curved. The lights, we foresaw, would become irresistible targets for dodgeball[1], and how long would the white walls remain pristine with 120 young people running around each week? And a curved hall, whilst maybe architecturally pleasing, was not practical for the many Scouting games and activities which involve running in a straight line. The floor in the old hall was concrete and therefore well able to withstand

---

[1] For those unfamiliar with Dodgeball as played by Scouts, it involves "throwers" hurling soft(ish) balls below the knees of the "dodgers" as they run around. If contact is made the "dodger" is out. We usually give Leaders the pleasure of throwing the balls at the Scouts. Leaders of course only try to aim below their knees. It's usually played as the last game of the evening.

the occasional slip of the axe or dropped knife during whittling practice. The new floor would be polished light oak. Yes, we saw a few issues...

But a solution was maybe to hand if we were prepared to be bold. Behind the church, still on its land, stood a single-storey block of three garages and two stores. We already used one of the stores for all of our Scouting equipment. The garages were used by the Parish clergy and the other store used by another Parish Group. Which led, on a damp September morning in 2011, to our own "What if" moment. *What if we added another floor over the garages and stores and used that for our own Scout Hall?* It helped that the question was considered by three people not averse to taking calculated risks. Looking at that fairly tatty garage block beside me (the Group Scout Leader and professional programme manager) stood David, (a property developer, serial enthusiast, and one of our committee members), and Tony (our Explorer Leader and born with Scouting in his veins). In true Scouting tradition we adjourned to the local pub to consider our "What if" question further.

Without being over-dramatic, the following few hours altered the course of our lives for the next four years and 17th Reigate's for the next fifty. Over a decent Thai curry and several pints purely to lubricate the brain cells, a basic plan of attack was thrashed out. Who would we need to convince? How much would it cost? Could the Group survive the process? As the brain-cells became more lubricated, the more we convinced ourselves that the idea would work.

Throughout the rest of this book I attempt to describe the course taken by the project. From fund-raising to finalization, the trials and tribulations, what worked, what didn't, and what we could have done differently. We all started cold with this project; none of us had much prior experience of fund-raising (at least on the scale needed) and for most of us, our building experience came from DIY projects around the house. So this book attempts to document some of the lessons we learned and might be useful to those considering a similar project, whether for a Scout Group, village hall, or other community venture. Inevitably we missed tricks along the way, but this is the story of four years of hard graft and ultimately, great reward. It demonstrates that with enough willpower and energy, a group of disparate volunteers can band together to create something special and it shows that the conventional way of approaching a construction project isn't the only route to success.

1 – GETTING STARTED

Any idea on the whole succeeds by convincing an increasing number of people that a) it's a good one, and b) it will work. But like an ember in a fire (to mix in an appropriate Scouting metaphor) an idea can get extinguished early on if someone chucks water over it or doesn't fan it at the right speed. So over our now-infamous Thai curry David, Tony, and I had drawn up a list of stakeholders – those who held the power to nurture the ember into flame or extinguish it completely. These were the people we needed to win over and convince. They included:

> ### What we were looking to build
>
> The proposal put to all of our stakeholders was as follows:
>
> - A 200m^2 multi-function hall with kitchen and washrooms.
> - A separate 30m^2 meeting room
> - Utilitarian finish which could withstand Scouts
> - Constructed over existing garages/stores
> - Separate entrance facilities, including disabled access
> - Expanded storage
> - Shared use by Parish and community
> - Built at no cost to Parish or Diocese

- The Parish, whose buildings we were proposing to re-develop
- The Diocese of Arundel and Brighton, the landlords who would need to grant us a lease
- Our Executive Committee, who would need to raise the money
- The parents of our young people, who would have to support the project in many ways
- Our young people, who would be involved in the fund-raising
- Bodies needing to give their statutory approval – for example the local Council for planning permission.

We recognized that the order in which we approached these was significant. For example, our Executive Committee could be as enthusiastic and bullish as they liked but if the Diocese refused a suitable lease then enthusiasm alone wouldn't save the day. And the Diocese would be unlikely to consider the idea if the Parish had thrown up its hands in horror at the notion. So it became pretty obvious to us that first we needed to convince the Parish that our idea had merit.

The Parish of the Nativity of the Lord, Redhill, comprises three churches with a combined congregation of around 2,000 Parishioners. Obviously we weren't going to lobby all of them individually. Pastoral care in the Parish most clearly belongs to the Clergy, but as in many Parishes, the management of its infrastructure – finances, buildings, social development and so on has devolved to a series of management committees. The Parish Priest relies on the wisdom and judgement of these committees for the day-to-day running of the Parish. The committees are "staffed", on a voluntary basis, usually by long-standing Parishioners (many retired) who often have relevant professional expertise to bring to the role and know how the land lies with Parish and Diocese. These committees, starting with the respective Chairs, were the ones we had to convince. So, to continue a theme, we invited them one at a time to the pub where we explained what we wanted to do.

Before each meeting we had done some homework. We knew one of the questions would be around how much the project would cost, so we had a back-of-envelope estimation of that. Another question would be where the money would come from, so we'd done a quick-and-dirty search about sources of funding. We'd also thought about what we wanted to get out of each meeting. Did they think this was a feasible idea, would they support the idea, and were any conditions attached? We also tailored the pitch according to whom we were meeting. For example, when talking to the Chair of the Building Development Committee we came from the angle that did the Parish really want 120 6-18 year-olds running around their nice shiny new Parish Centre each week? And would it be okay if we strung up wet tents in there to dry out (a not-infrequent requirement)? And if we were using it for three or four evenings each week then what availability would this leave for the rest of the Parish? When meeting the Chair of the Finance Committee, we changed the approach to emphasize that we could raise the money ourselves and that we wouldn't be looking for a sub from the Parish (although if they wanted to throw a few quid in our direction then we said we'd be fine about this).

This approach paid dividends. In a short space of time, for the cost of a few pints, we secured the unanimous backing and blessings of those we'd met. Had we not done this, and had we not done the corresponding homework beforehand, it is likely that our metaphoric ember of inspiration would have been permanently extinguished. A defining moment came in the unlikely setting of the Hampton Court Flower Show when I bumped into the daughter of a former Chair of the Finance Committee still heavily involved in the Parish and with his finger very much on the pulse. She said her dad thought this a fantastic idea, should have been done years ago, and to get on and make it happen. This was a pivotal moment which made us realize that actually we would succeed.

We are fortunate in our Parish to have Fr. Chris as the Parish Moderator, a former Scout himself, our biggest supporter in the Parish and great advocate for the Group and its young people. It was Fr. Chris who gave us our project name: "Building For The Future" – fitting both literally and figuratively. With the support of the various management committees under our belt, our conversation with him was both simple and positive. This was important since the next group we had to convince was the Diocesan Trustees and Fr. Chris was our link, spiritually and physically.

Getting a suitable lease

We knew that a suitable lease was a key to success. By "suitable" we meant long-duration (fifty years or more) and without any undue restrictions which would impinge on our Scouting activities. In the same way as the day-to-day administration of our Parish is handled by various management committees, the Diocese operates in a similar fashion but on a grander scale. The important one for us was the Finance Committee which controlled, amongst a lot of other things, administration of leases. But there is one significant difference from the way the Parish operates: as the Diocese is a charity in its own right then it also has a Board of Trustees, with members appointed by the Bishop and comprising a fairly even distribution of ordained ministers and lay members. Many of those were also members of the Finance Committee, which turned out to be most helpful. The Board of Trustees would need to give its approval for the project on the recommendation of the Finance Committee. Convincing the Finance Committee would put us well on the way to gaining Board of Trustee approval.

So we figured on a different plan of attack. Rather than focus on the adventurous side of Scouting and all of the excitement and opportunities it creates for young people, we came from the angle of what benefits our project would deliver to the Parish. In short, we approached it as if we were pitching a great business idea to potential investors, taking the emotion out of the argument and focusing instead on what the project would deliver.

The benefits we listed included:

- Creates opportunities to attract new members into the Parish and Church
- Gives a practical demonstration of the Diocese' support and commitment to its young Catholics
- Strengthens the connection between Scouting and the Catholic Church

And most importantly:

- More meeting space for Parish and community, at no cost to either

- More suited to less formal events (sub-text – a children's birthday party wouldn't trash the brand new Parish Centre)

We had been invited to present our case to the Finance Committee in person, so one morning I, in full uniform (complete with Kiro badge and necker in Papal yellow and white), David, Fr. Chris, and the Chair of the Parish Development Committee (a significant attendee since as well as being a great supporter of the project, he had substantial dealings with the Diocese during the construction of the new Parish Centre and thus knew "how things worked") were ushered into a relatively cramped room and invited to begin.

The Kiro badge

Sometimes it would have paid to do a bit more homework. As we left the meeting, the Chairman, a Monsignor, commented on how nice it was to see the Kiro badge on my uniform. Somewhat confused, I mumbled an appropriate response, and later admitted that 1) I'd only ever having heard it referred-to as "that Catholic badge" and thus I hadn't had a clue what the Monsignor was referring to, and 2) despite being a lifelong Catholic, the badge had only been sewn on the night before!

Our pitch, it has to be said, went very well. Questions were asked and answered, and it was apparent that we had judged the approach well: emphasizing the benefits to Catholic Scouting and the Parish was the right tack to take. Expecting to be told that a decision would be forthcoming, we were elated when at the end of the meeting the Chairman of the Finance Committee proposed to offer a 50-year lease which was met with unanimous approval from the other members present. The Board of Trustees approval followed shortly thereafter – we'd done it. Now we had to widen the ripples of support.

Convincing ourselves

We needed the backing of our Executive Committee, whose support around the fund-raising would be essential. There was a different set of factors to consider:

- What was the future of the Group if we did not go ahead with this project?
- Would the Group have the capacity to continue to deliver high-quality Scouting in parallel with the most ambitious project in its history?
- Did we have the skills – building, management, legal, etc. – for success?
- Would the project be affordable, both to build it and then to run it?

Our Group is very fortunate to have a strong Executive Committee headed by John, our Chairman and lifelong supporter of the Group. Presenting at my first Group AGM I compared John to a stick of Brighton rock – cut him in half and he would have 17th Reigate running through him top to toe. Our Executive Committee comprises former members and current parents, and has a breadth of Scouting and non-Scouting experience, a lot of it relevant to what we were proposing to do. John had been brought into the fold earlier so knew what was on the table.

We took the same approach as for the Diocese Finance Committee – a short presentation - but again changed the emphasis to suit the audience. This time we focused on the benefits for the Group, and in particular the first question above, i.e. what were the alternatives? Once it was acknowledged that really there were no practical alternatives and that without this project the future of the Group was at risk, acceptance of the idea became both inevitable and unanimous.

Convincing our members

Support from our young people was more or less a given – which Scout Group they attend is as much about where their friends go as the activities on offer and the fun they have. Whether we built the new hall or not was, for our young people, a rather moot point – as long as they had somewhere to meet then that was enough.

Support for the project from their parents was less assured but again was fundamental to success. Part of the Committee discussion had centred around how we would engage the parents and give them a sense of ownership in the project and responsibility for its completion. This was considered essential. The Committee was adamant that management and delivery of the project could not fall to "the usual culprits" – the 20% of volunteers found in almost every community organization who seem to end up doing 80% of the work. We needed parental buy-in from day-one.

The date was 6th January 2012 and on that evening we held an open meeting at a nearby church hall, advertising that an important announcement would be made about the future of 17th Reigate Scout Group. Now, whenever we have held an AGM without the attraction of "entertainment" by each Section, optimistically we set out dozens of chairs only to find that maybe half of the first two rows are occupied (and on one infamous occasion when it was lashing down with rain, the AGM was held in the bar of the old hall and attendance was so pitiful that everyone fitted around a small table). So we didn't have especially high hopes about a good attendance. As it turned out, our pessimism was misplaced – the place was rammed and people were standing. Around 80% of our parents attended – enough for a convincing vote one way or the other.

Another presentation, again modified from the Diocese Finance Committee one, formed the basis of the meeting. But again we changed the emphasis and also jazzed it up bit:

- We gave a brief lesson on the history of the Group
- We showed how the Group had grown, both in membership and range of activities
- We explained the gist of the proposal, an idea of its costs and where the money would come from, and showed an artist's impression of the planned new building
- <u>We explained how this would benefit their children</u>
- We told them how they would need to be involved from the start and asked them to sign up for help in specific areas (we had pre-printed forms)
- We explained that we were looking for their support, by way of a vote, for a detailed three-month feasibility study.
- We said we'd hold another meeting following completion of the feasibility study, when we would ask for the green light to proceed.

Two things came from this meeting.

1) Overwhelming support from all parents at the meeting. In fact, the vote would have been unanimous bar one abstainer. We had what we wanted: the go-ahead to proceed with the feasibility study.

2) A group of our Explorers came forward to offer to do a sponsored hike to kick-start the fund-raising. More on this later, but another defining moment for the project. If we'd been able to convince a group of teenagers of the merits of the project and to do something about it unprompted then success was assured.

The feasibility study

With parental support for the three-month feasibility study given so robustly, we needed to deliver. We'd set out its scope as follows:

- Confirmation of the estimated build-costs

- Availability of external funding such that Group funding would not be more than 15% of the total
- Running-costs could be met through normal fund-raising
- The project would receive the necessary consents
- The Group could survive the project

Estimated build costs

17th Reigate is a large Scout Group – 130 young people provide a wide pool of parents and family members with a diverse mix of jobs, skills, and interests. We were fortunate that we had Paul, one of our parents who ran a construction management company. After suitable bribing with beer, he offered to lend a hand with the estimating the construction costs and later found us most of the sub-contractors we needed. The box "Headings used for Costings" shows how the project was broken down. Against each of these we allocated costs indicating best and worst cases.

We used the three months available for the feasibility study to get costs as accurate as possible:

Headings used for costings	
1	Demolitions
2	Site setup & preliminaries.
3	Foundations
4	Estimated utilities fees
5	Underground drainage
6	Sleeving for services
7	Brickwork to DPC
8	Concrete slab for entire footprint
9	Brickwork structure
10	Structural steelwork package
11	First floor structure
12	Supply and fit of doors and windows.
13	Supply of roof structure
14	Supply and fit of new roof covering
15	Supply and installation of all fascia, soffits, gutters & downpipes
16	Supply and fit of fire escape
17	Wall, Floor ceiling insulation
18	First fix carpentry /boxings etc.
19	First / Second Fix electrics
20	First / Second Fix plumbing and heating.
21	Dry Lining and plastered finishes
22	Floor Finishes
23	Kitchen
24	Supply and fit lift
25	Second Fix carpentry
26	Toilet supply cost as a pack.
27	Internal decorations
28	Professional fees

- Some of the costs were based on industry knowledge
- For specialist items such as the disabled lift, quotes were obtained
- Assumptions were made about the use of voluntary labour and donations in kind
- Assumptions were made about the level of possible supplier discounts.

We also investigated and changed the proposed method of construction. Originally seen as a simple extension over existing buildings, it became apparent that the existing foundations would not support a first-floor without underpinning and that the simpler and cheaper way would be to demolish and build new. This had two other advantages: we could change the footprint to give a better shape, and being a new build would qualify it for zero-rating for VAT purposes, thus offering a substantial cost-saving.

The conclusion, for the purposes of the feasibility study, was that the original back-of-envelope estimate on construction costs was about right (in fact we ended up quite a bit adrift for fairly valid reasons, but this is covered in more detail in Chapter 5 – Getting It Built).

Availability of external funding.

Our "quick and dirty" look at external sources of funding centred mainly on a list provided by the Scout Association HQ at Gilwell. This, I was cheerily assured on a phone call with them, represented really good sources of funding and that a success-rate of 50% was readily achievable. In fact, the reality was rather different. Researching further the organizations on their list showed that for the majority, we wouldn't qualify for the grants, either geographically, or because they did not support capital build projects, or (unbelievably given the origin of the list) they did not support youth organizations.

A different approach was needed. Given that we were fund-raising virgins, at least for the amount we needed, a search of Amazon for books relating to "raising funds for community projects" and that ilk showed others had not only done the same but also helpfully had written it down. A literary investment was made and a series of mostly useful books arrived through the post. (The titles are included in the Bibliography). Through one of these we were introduced to Funding Central – a free database of UK grant-making bodies. This, we found, was a much richer sea in which to trawl.

Chapter 4 goes into far more detail about how we used this information to provide the funds we needed. However, for the feasibility study we restricted ourselves to a search for suitable funders and a coarse sieving for prospective sources.

Our search criteria yielded about 600 grant-awarding organizations, and the sieving left about 100 in the "looks promising" or "promising but not yet" categories. Further research gave an idea of the likely amounts of funding to be offered. Totting this up, and applying an average success rate of 10% (more realistic, according to the books I had read), showed that enough external funding should be available to achieve what we'd set out to build. This was sufficient for the feasibility study.

Our coarse sieving criteria

For those interested in following the same approach, the search criteria we used initially on Funding Central are given on page 84

All of the results were printed out, reviewed one by one, and categorized into

1) Not a chance (we failed the criteria)
2) Possible but unlikely (only tenuous connection to our cause)
3) Looks promising (we met most or all of published criteria)
4) Promising, but not yet (outside the timetable for application)

Internal fund-raising

Here we were on more familiar ground. 17th Reigate, as with most Scout Groups, has undertaken regular fund-raising to pay for new or replacement equipment, to subsidize Group activities, to pay for transport and so on. Our own fund-raising was mostly centred around Christmas activities and a big firework display in the church grounds in November (aside – ironically as a Catholic Group, we'd always built a massive bonfire for 5th November and would proudly cremate not one, but four Guys made by our Cubs from old pyjamas stuffed with straw and paper plates for faces. Although very popular and pretty lucrative, this may have contributed to the Parish's decision to build its new Centre on the site of our bonfire, thus relegating our somewhat anti-Papist firework display to history).

For the feasibility study the calculation and evaluation of internal fund-raising was fairly easy. We capped the amount of funding we'd need to raise ourselves to 15% of project costs so that it wouldn't become a millstone around our necks (it did, but more of that later). With a firm estimate of project costs, 15% translated into a definite amount and a review of our fund-raising track-record for the past few years showed that, with a modest increase in effort (it didn't turn out like that, but more of that later), we should comfortably hit that target.

It is worth noting that in reality we probably did not need to include <u>any</u> internal fund-raising towards the target – we could have found an extra 15% through additional grant applications. But the main reason we did it was to give a sense of ownership to our young people and their parents. We reasoned that if they had to graft for some of the funds then they were more likely to be motivated and get behind the project and contribute, especially in the latter stages when we would be looking for practical as well as financial support. As we will see, this was the correct decision and yielded some imaginative and (for us) new ways of raising funds and, later, plenty of help painting.

Estimated running costs

These were probably the hardest to estimate with any confidence of accuracy. We reasoned that they would comprise:

- Insurances
- Rates
- A sinking fund for maintenance
- Utility bills

We also needed to factor in the normal Group business-as-usual (BAU) running costs for membership of the UK Scout Association, equipment and so on. Although not part of the building running costs, these costs would still need to be met.

We could reasonably estimate insurances, rates, and the sinking fund. We were obliged to take out building insurance via the Diocese, so knowing the re-build cost (to be based on, as the-then Diocese Finance Secretary put it, a proper building process, not mates' rates) this cost would be accurately predictable. Being a charitable body, a discussion with the local Council indicated we would qualify for a discretionary discount on rates. The amount we set aside in a sinking-fund for future maintenance would be under our control. The real unknown would be the cost for utilities – gas, water, electricity, and internet access.

On the other side of the P&L we would have income from fund-raising (estimated based on track record) and surplus from annual subs. We could also set a reasonable expectation of additional donations from loaning the hall for community use at times when not needed by 17th Reigate (for example, daytime and most weekends). The going rate for similar local facilities was a matter of simple research, and we made an assumption about what level of occupancy would be both achievable and manageable.

So a certain amount of cost analysis was done. Knowing what our likely annual income would be, and subtracting from it the estimated total of insurances, rates, the sinking-fund, and BAU costs left us with an annual amount we'd need to find which to cover utilities. We were comfortable that utility costs could be met from this amount and concluded that for the feasibility study, we could tick this off as achievable.

Planning consent

We needed to establish early on whether we would hit any obstacles with planning permission. Being great believers in the power of face-to-face communications, David and I arranged to meet one of the District Planning Officers to look over our plans. Time well-spent as we were told that in principle there would be no objection, but we were advised to be mindful of aesthetic considerations due to the building's proximity to St. Joseph's Church, which had won designs for its architectural merit. A design sympathetic in appearance and material would, we were told, be a requirement from the District Conservation Officer – and indeed in due course we had to account for this in the design. But generally the news was what we wanted to hear – nothing obvious to get in the way of a successful planning application.

Reigate District Scouts

As the second-largest (at the time) Group in Reigate District Scouts, we felt it both incumbent on us, and out of courtesy, to share our plans early on with District. After all, if the project failed or got into hot water financially, there would be a negative, rather than positive, impact on local Scouting. So we gave the District Commissioner the usual (by now) spiel and received the expected green light, as far as District was concerned, to press ahead. In fact, there was a postscript to this at the District AGM the following year when by a unanimous vote, the annual District Shield was awarded to 17th Reigate for, as the District Commissioner put it, "not only growing the Group but doing so whilst pursuing their crazy idea of building their own hall!"

Network Rail

This was a worry we needed to address. We would be building alongside the London to Brighton train line and Network Rail's Asset Protection team exists to prevent projects from compromising its infrastructure. This isn't to say Network Rail can stop a project on a whim, but it can insist on all manner of safeguards and risk assessments being in place for construction to move forward. All of which have to be paid for by the customer and which, during a phone call with them to establish process, would more likely cost thousands of pounds than hundreds. All we could do with this information at this stage was to add a further contingency to the project budget.

Later on, the outcome of this ended up in our favour. Once we had submitted our plans for inspection, Network Rail concluded that we were building just beyond the minimum acceptable distance from a live rail and therefore they had no interest. We're still not sure what type of tape-measure they used, but were grateful that it must have been made of rubber. We had dodged the first of several bullets; Network Rail gave its consent for us to proceed without it costing us a penny extra.

Other consultations

In hindsight there were other consultations we should have made earlier, but through lack of experience, didn't.

- We should have looked closer into the provision of utilities. Our assumption had been that we could tap into existing supplies feeding the church. For water we found we needed a new independent supply as we were categorized as a new build. We also ended up installing a new electricity supply.

- Main drainage. Our construction took place at the lowest point on the church site, so rainwater and foul drainage were always going to be problematic. Our options became further restricted when we found there were regulations around the maximum angle of fall to connect into a main drain. There's more about this in Chapter 5 – Getting It Built.

- Changes in building regulations meant we needed to put in a vast amount more steel to stiffen the building then we'd originally allowed. This cost us both more money and time. Knowing earlier wouldn't have changed the requirements but would have increased the funds we had to raise before construction started.

Would the Group survive the project?

"The operation was a success but the patient died" was the analogy I used at the parents' meeting on 6th January 2012. By which I meant that we didn't want to find that on completion of the project, we'd taken our eye off the ball and the Group had withered away in the meantime. This wasn't an inconceivable scenario: as part of our funding research we had talked to a local Group which had spent fifteen years raising money for its new HQ, eventually completed it and six months later the Group was in dire straits. The trap they'd fallen into was to use the same people to drive the project as who also ran the Sections, i.e. the Leaders – putting an eventually unsustainable load onto those who are, after all, volunteers. Something had to give, and what gave way was the entire Group.

The secret to avoiding this pitfall was, we felt, the way we organized ourselves and to ensure that there was a clear divide between Leaders and helpers running the Sections, and the management of the project.

We came up with a structure we felt would work to manage the project without impinging on the Scouting activities. This is shown on the next page and existed in parallel with the normal Group structure of Group Scout Leader, Section Leaders and helpers. By and large this worked although on occasion there were bigger overlaps than we'd have wished for. Fortunately, we are blessed with a dedicated and motivated bunch of volunteers and to their credit it cost us nothing more than a few grumbles, mostly from other halves.

Building	Fund-raising	Legal	Comms
Responsible for • Design • Plans • Costs • Permissions • Management of build	Responsible for • Grant applications • Project fund-raising events and opportunities • Fund-raising for normal Group running costs	Responsible for • Lease/licence • Other 3rd party interests • Ongoing responsibilities	Responsible for • Publicity • Parish liaison • Progress reports • Consistency
Governance and administration Responsible for Project controls, project finances, project decision-making			

Mostly our Executive Committee member volunteers gravitated to their natural comfort zones. David managed actual building process and one of Tony's fortes is to come up with imaginative ways to extract money legally from people – he led the fund-raising sub-committee. One of our Committee members is a government lawyer so could obviate the need for separate legal advice around the lease, saving us thousands of pounds in the process. I, as Group Scout Leader, had a foot in both project and Group running. With a vested interest in completing the project to allow the Group to flourish, and to ensure that my patient did indeed remain alive throughout the operation, I together with other Committee members ended up doing a lot of the governance and administration piece, reporting into the Executive Committee as required. This had the advantage of ensuring a good flow of communications across the whole Group structure.

Another advantage of this structure was that it devolved decision-making to where it was needed. Determined to avoid constricting the project by insisting on decision-by-committee, we gave autonomy to the work-streams to decide as they saw fit. Thus the fund-raising sub-committee could decide themselves which fund-raising activities the Group would undertake, and inform the Executive Committee. The Building sub-committee decided on all matters to do with the actual construction, including spending whatever needed to be spent on materials or services. The only time anything would be referred back to the Executive Committee was if a fundamental change was needed likely to affect either overall budget or timescales. For those familiar with project-management this is the RACI (Responsible, Accountable, Consulted, Informed) concept. We just didn't get around to writing it in its normal matrix format.

This structure worked well from the start and evolved over time as more people became involved and additional support was co-opted.

Green for Go

As we'd promised the parents, we held a follow-up meeting after three months to present the conclusions of the feasibility study. We adopted a simpler structure – a recap of what we said we'd find out, and the results of that research. Although less well-attended than the first one, we had enough present to call for a vote on whether or not to proceed. This time there were no abstainers – the decision to proceed was unanimous and had taken less than an hour. Now the hard work started.

In conclusion, what did we learn?

Ideas may start small but will grow through careful nurturing

Our vision would have withered on the vine had it not been developed by like-minded individuals and a plan of attack developed for it to gain wider approval

Know the stakeholders – those individuals or groups who need to be convinced and remain on-side

We identified early those people who needed to back the idea, and we had a plan to lobby them specifically and individually. We carefully mapped out the order in which we approached them.

Explain the idea carefully and clearly and don't assume everyone has the same level of passion about it.

We couldn't assume that everyone has the knowledge of what modern Scouting is about. Nor could we assume that their own Scouting experience had been positive!

Tailor the approach and be professional

From the outset we focused on the benefits of the project, choosing which to emphasize depending on the audience. We delivered with passion rather than emotion. This approach continued through our fund-raising, especially when preparing grant applications.

There's no such thing as too much research

We could have and should have spent longer on some aspects of the feasibility study, especially around

cost estimates. This wouldn't have changed the decision to proceed but would have given fewer surprises and sleepless nights in the latter stages of the project.

Clarify the VAT position

If there is a plan to reclaim any VAT, then discuss this beforehand with HMRC and get a written ruling from them confirming eligibility and caveats. VAT regulations are complex and dynamic, and getting the situation clarified upfront can save a lot of pain later.

Proper organization is essential

Had we not separated project from Scouting then we could have had real issues with continuing to deliver outstanding Section programmes. But by letting people settle in their own comfort zones to deliver parts of the project meant we were not trying to hammer square pegs into round holes.

Avoid decision-by-committee

If we'd insisted that every decision was referred back to the Executive Committee for endorsement, then the committee would have been mired in permanent meetings and nothing would have got done. From the start there had to be a large element of trust and confidence that everyone knew what they were doing and thus were empowered for local decision-making.

Define the success factors and know what success looks like

In lobbying stakeholders, we had a firm idea in our heads what we wanted out of each meeting: preferably unqualified support but if support was qualified then what were the caveats.

2 - PLANNING TO RAISE THE MONEY

The first meeting of our fund-raising sub-committee was held, where else, but in a local pub. Here we spent a convivial couple of hours mapping out where we thought the money would come from and evolving an embryonic fund-raising plan. It was pretty clear from the start that we wouldn't build a new Scout Hall by selling teas and coffees after Sunday Mass and that some hefty sources of income would be needed.

Our fund-raising sub-committee continued to meet every few weeks throughout the lifetime of the project, and still continues to meet as we raise funds to operate the building. Its attendance ebbed and flowed but as is so often the case there was a hard-core of people who saw their contribution as a means to reach the end quicker and thus get their lives back. What became obvious at that first meeting was that:

- We had some pretty creative thinkers among us
- We weren't afraid of trying new ideas

These were important attributes – they ensured that fund-raising didn't become stale and remained profitable. The sub-committee focussed mostly on the internal fund-raising (there is a comment further down on how we went about applying for grants) as these events required most organization.

We set the expectation to start construction after we had raised 90% of the funding. We felt that once local suppliers and other funders saw that the project was real and construction had started then the remaining 10% would be readily forthcoming. This is broadly what happened, though we had to scrabble around for a lot more than the last 10% as our building costs increased. More on this in Chapter 5. At the parental meeting on 6th January 2012 I had said that, given the funding which seemed to be available, we could easily achieve our target in two years. Turned out that no-one at the meeting actually believed this but they were kind enough not to question my sanity (at least in public) and went along with it. But… this is where I enter the smug zone. On 7th January 2014 – exactly two years <u>and one day</u> after the first meeting – we announced we'd reached the 90% threshold. I can safely say that as a professional project manager, none of my projects have ever achieved that level of accuracy! To raise that amount of money (and we are talking well into six figures) so quickly was, we were told by several professional bodies, almost unprecedented for a bunch of amateurs and remains a testament to the professionalism, commitment, and dedication of all involved.

I have given below the targets from that first meeting along with (in parenthesis) an estimation of what we actually achieved.

Grants	70%	(64%)
In-house fund-raising	15%	(14%)
In-kind funding	10%	(3%)
Individual donations	5%	(2%)
Loans	0%	(17%)

By "in-kind funding" we meant donations of goods or services instead of hard cash. It is difficult to represent accurately the total value of this since much was based on heavily discounted prices which hid the true benefit of the goods or services. The actual cost saving was almost certainly well in excess of the 3% figure shown above. Also loosely into this area would fall the volunteer labour we would use when we got to the internal fit-out and decoration. In a total-cost model we would have ascribed a value to this "free" labour, however we didn't bother as we had not included these costs in the project budget – we assumed (correctly) this work would get done for free.

Gift Aid would be another source of income as during the project lifetime HMRC changed the rules around allowing Gift Aid to be reclaimed on small cash donations (so-called bucket collections). We did not factor this into our fund-raising target as it was very difficult to predict and ultimately would be of modest value.

As we went along we refined the structure of our fund-raising organization. Recognizing that applying for grants would better suit the responsibility of just one or two people (for consistency) whereas organizing say a fund-raising social complete with food and entertainment would involve many more people, we expanded our sub-committee so that we had the right level of resources in each area. Again, people gravitated to their areas of comfort.

Also put in place was a mechanism to track results. A spreadsheet was created by our Treasurer with worksheets loosely following the above structure. This was used to record income generated from all fund-raising and in it we also included pledges – promises of future funding whose release was dependent on criteria not yet satisfied but expected to be. To ensure separation between Group running costs and building costs a separate bank account was used. This meant we always had an accurate picture of what we had raised (and later, had spent) which reconciled against our tracking spreadsheet. Once a month I would meet with our Treasurer and John, our Chairman to go through the Group and project finances to make sure everything had been properly allocated. As a process this worked well.

It's worth noting that we did briefly consider the use of professional fund-raisers – a local school had used this approach very successfully to raise money for a new sports hall. But some investigation suggested that this was not a cheap option (with investment needed up-front), the results were not guaranteed (thus might cost us more than it raised), and the timetable would not be within our control (we wouldn't be able to predict when building could start). Better, we thought, to do it ourselves, in keeping with our approach to the rest of the project and our somewhat gung-ho Scouting attitude.

To use a jigsaw analogy at this stage we now had the corners and sides in place – a plan, a structure, some targets, and a way to track results. Next we needed to fill in the middle by generating cash.

3 – PUTTING THE FUN IN FUNDRAISING

This chapter deals with our own internal fund-raising – how we raised 15% of the cost ourselves and what we had to do to achieve it. It describes the funding events and methods we used – many will be familiar to Scout Groups but there are some more oddball ones among them. Also described are some fund-raising events which we thought about but for various reasons didn't do – these are included at the end in case they inspire others.

Our internal fund-raising was, from the start, under the control of our fund-raising sub-committee. In reality the sub-committee spent far more of its time discussing the 15% internal target than the 85% from elsewhere since these events required much more organization and people to contribute.

Early on we tried to introduce the concept of "soup to nuts" responsibility. In essence, anyone was free to propose any fund-raising idea they liked but they then had to take responsibility for owning it and seeing it through end-to-end or in meal terms, from the soup starter course to the post-prandial nuts. Didn't mean they had to do everything – they could coerce and co-opt others as needed but having voiced the idea in the first place, they couldn't simply pass the baton to someone else. Along with this was the concept of a target outcome and post-event feedback. The target may be solely financial – an amount to be raised by a specific event – or a combination of financial and intangible –for example, increased awareness of the project. And post-event feedback was supposed to improve quality and outcome should we repeat the event.

Neither of these lasted particularly long, in fact the soup-to-nuts concept stuck permanently at the entrée without so much as a single crouton in sight. As worthy as the idea was it became simpler for the sub-committee to get on and plan the events en masse rather than to execute a management consultancy-style process. Likewise, the post-event feedback became rather redundant – common sense told us which events worked well without a bunch of analysis and those that didn't work weren't repeated.

We were also conscious to try to avoid targeting the same audience for each event. Donor or compassion fatigue is a real phenomenon and we didn't want our supporters to think we were continually hitting only on them and thus become disenchanted with the whole project.

It's also worth noting that for some of the activities described below, the sole purpose wasn't just to make money. Many had a dual purpose to raise awareness within the Parish and local community of what we were doing and how far we'd got. The Public Relations element was often worth more than the money the event brought in – it generated goodwill and ensured that the support we received both inside the Group and outside remained solid.

The events below are described in no particular order. An indicator of financial return is given but citing exact amounts raised is avoided for obvious reasons.

Explorers' hike from Brownsea Island

Immediately after our parental meeting to kick off the project, six of our Explorers came forward to offer to do a sponsored hike from Brownsea Island, the site of the first-ever Scout camp, back to the garages in Redhill which would be torn down to make way for our new Scout Hall. The reason they gave was entirely and commendably selfless: as one they explained that because they'd each got a lot out of Scouting then they wanted to be able to give something back to the Group. This was the Scouting ethos made real and made us, as a Group, incredibly proud of them. It proved a bonding experience for them, too. Even though they have long-since left the Group they remain very close; friendships which existed before their hike were strengthened and new bonds were formed.

The hike required a large degree of organization which they mostly did by themselves. The distance was around 180 kilometres and we suggested they planned to complete the walk over five days. Logistics played an important part and again the familial value of Scouting came to the fore as all of the overnight accommodation was offered for free either in Scout Halls belonging to Groups along the route or nearby camp-sites. We gave them a goody-bag of souvenirs – our Group scarf and badges and a few other bits and pieces – to leave with their hosts by way of a thank-you. By coincidence our Group summer camp that year was planned for the New Forest, which made getting them to the starting point simple. We had a Group day exploring Brownsea Island and everyone on our camp was able to wave them off as they boarded the ferry to Sandbanks.

They accomplished the hike with flying colours. Despite horrendous blisters for some of them, blazing hot weather and torrential

Happy vs. grumpy

Although they had done a lot of short hikes, none of our super six had experience of walking many kilometres day after day. This, we warned them, would be the toughest part.

I sketched out a simple graph showing how their emotions may vary day-by-day, and that the timing of who felt what when would be different for all of them. The idea was to forewarn them and encourage them to look out for, and motivate, each other. This graph became known as "Mike's Happy/Grumpy Chart" which to my surprise they did look at and heed: "what does Mike's Richter Scale of happiness say we should be feeling today" one of them was heard to say on their video diary.

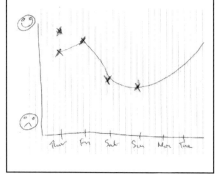

downpours, encounters with snakes, and occasional issues with navigation they made it back on time. There was a welcoming party in the local park with a photographer from the local newspaper and then they walked the last mile before shucking off their rucksacks and kicking the garage door to mark the end. If we were proud of them for coming up with the idea in the first place, then we were doubly so when they completed what they'd set out to do. In achieving their goal, they raised well over £5,000 in sponsorship which kick-started our fund-raising in the best way imaginable. The event remains an inspiration to our young people and one of the highlights of the whole project.

Bag packing

Tell most adult volunteers in Scouting that another bag-packing session is planned and you are likely to hear a chorus of groans. Tell most of the kids and there's often more enthusiasm. I'm one of the rarities – an adult who actually doesn't mind doing it. I think it puts Scouting on public display and it is extremely beneficial for the social development of our young people for them to actively engage with members of the public in a day-to-day activity. And it's an activity in which young people cannot simply remain mute or distract themselves on a mobile phone – they actually have to talk to people, to interact and socialize. Of course, it also helps that bag-packing is extremely lucrative and, for effort versus reward, easily the most profitable way we have found to raise funds.

For those readers who have never been accosted at a supermarket checkout by a youth wearing a Scout uniform demanding "help packing your bags?", the premise is simple. We position one or two of our young people by each checkout and they help, if the customer agrees, to load the groceries into bags and place them into their trollies. There's an adjacent bucket into which the customer can throw a donation of change. And that, pretty much, is all there is to it. What makes it especially lucrative when our Group does bag-packing is that we deploy our secret weapon – one so powerful that customers seldom leave the checkout without a donation and more often than not, pay us not to pack their bags. So, what is our weapon of choice? We send in the Beavers! We have found that the cutie factor of a six- or seven-year old beaming up, barely tall enough to see over the top of the checkout surface, becomes irresistible and our takings multiply accordingly. It gets even better if we pair a small Beaver with a tall Scout or Explorer. Somehow this enhances the "ahhh sweet" factor whilst giving the customer a modicum of assurance that their eggs or tomatoes won't be packed with a bag of spuds on top of them.

Mostly we bag-pack around Christmas-time when there are heavily-laden trollies coming through and generally people are more generous in both spirit and with their loose change. We provide our young people (and adults) with an array of obligatory festive headwear, including some animatronic hats which give the appearance that the wearer has a live ferret on his/her head. These always get a laugh (at least, until the accompanying music drives the checkout assistant insane and they request the hat to be switched off). Bag-packing is done in shifts of two hours according to a pre-arranged rota– plenty long enough for the Beavers who tend to flag after 60-90 minutes – and if we have enough conscripts then we're in position before the tills open and stay until the last customer is through. We also insist that our young people and uniformed Leaders all wear full uniform and frequently remind them (mostly the young people) that their trousers won't fall down if they remove their hands from their pockets.

There are often memorable moments. The following names have been changed to protect the innocent.

Christmas trollies often contain a wide variety of fruit and vegetables. So if I'm supervising a checkout where we've stationed one or two of our Beavers then occasionally I'll test them to see how many types of fruit or vegetable they recognize as they pack them. I figure that bag-packing may as well be educational. The common ones – spuds, carrots, apples, oranges et cetera are all recognized without problem. Sometimes they get some of the more exotic or less-common ones too – aubergines, kiwi-fruit, beetroots and so on. Last Christmas, predictably a bag of loose Brussel sprouts came through. "What are these?", I asked Jimmy, who was seven. "They're sprouts", he replied before explaining to the customer, "I love sprouts, they make me trump really loudly".

On another occasion we had one of our Cubs helping. Tom was a child with various learning difficulties, a consequence of which was that he was very tactile – he liked to pick things up and feel their texture and shape. This particular time Tony, our Explorer Leader, was helping him pack the bags. Or rather, Tony was packing the bags whilst Tom, to the alarm of the customer, was picking up each item from the conveyor belt and sniffing it vigorously before passing it to Tony. Didn't matter what it was – toiletries, fruit, cakes, a bag of lettuce – all had to pass the Tom sniff-test before it could be packed. Things took an even more bizarre twist when I heard Tony shouting. I looked round to see him in high-speed pursuit after Tom who was heading into the nearby café, laughing and running away with a customer's pizza in his hands. After a brief tussle both pizza and Cub were returned undamaged; fortunately, the customer although a little miffed, saw the funny side.

We also get a lot of comments – mostly very complimentary – from customers as they pass the Leaders on the way out. The following are genuine (I wrote them down at the time).

Customer: "Who's that boy at the end – the one with the ginger hair?"

Us: "Oh that's Percy. What's he done now?"

Customer: "He's been really helpful and we've been having a really good conversation. He made me laugh – he's been critiquing all of my shopping, telling me what he liked, didn't like, and what I should have bought instead. All his mate did was pack a jar of Marmite."

And some more:

Customer: "We had to tell him where to put a couple of things"

Customer: "Gives them a great incentive to study hard else they could end up doing this all the time"

Customer:	"Nice to see Cubs and Scouts, I had two helping" (then he illustrated this by sticking up two fingers)
Customer:	"There were some girls in uniform down there"
Us:	"Yes, girls have been able to join Scouts for some years now"
Customer:	"(Harrumph) Different in my day, whatever next"

Sometimes we received donations other than money. As well as the inevitable handful of foreign coins and buttons, we have received doughnuts, some chocolate buttons, and a fingernail. And from one lady a £5 note with explicit instructions to buy a tin of sweets for the kids "to keep their energy up".

After the tills have closed and our buckets retrieved, we'd adjourn to someone's house, break out the sloe gin, and count the money. Counting many hundreds of pounds of change (yes it is that lucrative) does take a while since it has to be bagged into the right amount per denomination. When it's all done and someone has lugged it to the bank the next day (and it helps to forewarn the bank that this is arriving else a long queue of irate customers tends to build behind you if you simply dump it on the counter) then we breathe a sigh of relief... until the next time.

Plant sale

This was one of our earliest initiatives in our fund-raising campaign and one, we felt, which ticked the boxes of getting our young people involved early. Like bag-packing, the premise was simple. Get the kids to grow some plants from seeds and then, a few months later, hold a plant sale after one of the busier church services. To make it really simple to achieve, in February a couple of volunteers spent ages assembling kits comprising seeds (donated by local garden centres), lollypop sticks for labelling, soil, and instructions. All that needed to be added were suitable containers, water, and a sunny windowsill. We also introduced the incentive of a prize for growing the tallest sunflower. An indicator of the popularity of the venture, the prize went unclaimed.

We did eventually get enough plants to sell but it was hard work. One of the problems we faced was not knowing how things were going (or rather, growing). We had to take it on trust that a) the seeds had been planted, b) they had been planted in time for a visible result to have appeared by the date of the plant sale, c) that the seedling would be nurtured and cared-for and thus appear vaguely healthy, and d) we would have a reasonable variety of plants – flowers, herbs, and vegetables – to sell. In the end we had a pretty good selection although there was a deep suspicion that some parents

17th Reigate (St. Joseph's) Scout Group

Vegetables, herbs, flowers, bedding plants, annuals, Perennials... you name it, our Beavers, Cubs, Scouts, and Explorers have been growing them from seeds over the last couple of months and the results are now ready for you to buy!

Growing our funds! Our first-ever plant sale

St. Joseph's Church
Sunday 6th May
after 8.30am and
10.30am Masses

Carry-to-car service available for bulk purchases!

had nipped down to the garden centre the day before the plant sale, re-potted some purchased marigolds or chives into a few yoghurt pots recovered from their recycling bin, and sent them in as "home grown".

We augmented the plant sale, which was held in a large marquee outside the church, with bacon sandwiches and a home-made cake sale. These made almost as much as selling the plants. We made a few hundred quid overall but afterwards the consensus was that the labour and stress of getting everything ready both to grow and then to sell significantly outweighed the financial return. This was one idea which we chose not to repeat.

Parish and Group Socials

Over the four years of the project we ran a lot of social events. We continue to organize these post-project as they fall plumb into the "dual purpose" category mentioned earlier. The financial return versus effort to stage isn't fantastic but the goodwill generated by putting on an event which draws the community together is immeasurable. Modesty apart, we've become pretty good at organizing these and attendees have a good time at a reasonable ticket price, which encourages them to come to the next one. The list below isn't exhaustive but indicates the range of social events we've staged:

- Autumn Barn Dance
- London Surprise Night
- Jazz on a Summer's evening
- Burns Night (three years running)
- Christmas Cheer
- St. George's Curry and Quiz Night

The format is similar for each.

- We sell adult tickets and discounted tickets for a family
- There is usually live music
- There is always a raffle
- Tables/chairs are set out and decorated, along with the hall, in an appropriate theme so the venue looks attractive
- A two-course meal is always provided, often served to the tables
- There is usually a bar

Following this formula has meant that pretty much every event we've staged has been a sell-out. Take Burns Night as an example. This comes complete with a piper addressing the Haggis for which we supply guests with a tot of whisky, the meal comprises the normal mashed tatties, neeps, and the ubiquitous Haggis, and there's a band calling a ceilidh. Given that we're about as far from Scotland as one can get in this country, I was concerned that repeating this year after year would wear a bit thin and we'd see a decline in attendance. I couldn't have been more wrong – the third year was the most well-attended with the best rate of (financial) return yet – another sell-out despite an increase in ticket price. It would seem, from talking to guests and listening to some of the feedback, that the reason for the event (celebrating the life of Rabbie Burns) or the cause of the event (17th Reigate still needing to raise money to pay off its debts) are not why it is so popular. It's more because it fulfils a social gap; it provides a local event which all generations can enjoy and see familiar faces and meet old friends whilst being fed and entertained at reasonable cost.

It's worth saying a bit about the organization which goes with these events. Again taking our Burns Night Supper and Ceilidh as an example, the running-order went something as follows:

Year in advance:	Hall and band booked. Many of our socials utilized musical talent available within the Parish and therefore the latter wasn't always needed
Two months in advance:	Advanced notification "date for your diaries" style via Sections and Parish newsletters
One month in advance:	Ticket sales start – usually with one person coordinating to prevent over-selling. Usually we have a cap of around 150 tickets due to the size of venue. Depending on the type of event we have found the school playground to be an especially rich market for ticket sales.
	Detailed planning: who will be responsible for shopping, setting out tables, decorating, preparing food, cooking, serving, clearing up, running the bar and other minutiae.
The week before:	Shopping for food (in the case of our Burns Night this included purchasing an inordinate number of swedes and bulk-ordering Haggis)

| | Getting pots, pans, etc. from Scout store and sourcing anything missing. |

On the day: Food preparation team – peeling, chopping, wrapping (Haggis)

Hall team – laying out tables and chairs, decorating tables, assembling stage

Cooking team – boiling, mashing, unwrapping (Haggis), sampling

Serving team – plating up, serving to tables, clearing tables

Washer-uppers – washing up, repatriating pots and pans

Anyone still standing – clearing the hall at end of evening

As can be surmised, there is a lot of hard work involved in staging these events. We are fortunate to have a fantastic cooking team who can turn their hand to many types of cuisine and serve good-quality hot food for an amazingly low cost. We are equally fortunate to have a large pool of Executive Committee members, Section Leaders, and parents who step in on the day of the event to assist with the many other jobs. This usually means we can spread the tasks around although this never stops us from moaning afterwards that more help was needed and "we're never going to do this again". We always do: the benefits, both financial and intangible, are too great to ignore.

Raffles (including a prize draw)

I have included raffles separately as they are a consistent component of many of our events. These are "on the day" raffles, for which no licence is needed and rely on selling numbered tickets to an in-situ audience. We usually co-opt our Explorers to do the actual selling at the event since it gets them mingling with the crowd. Then we usually get them to fold up all of the tickets since it is a very boring job.

The prizes have always been donated, meaning the return on the raffle is 100% profit. We're constantly seeking new raffle prizes, and unwanted presents post-Christmas are always a good source (though embarrassing if the donor is the one to then win it back). Another good source is free gifts - one stationery supplier routinely awards gifts commensurate with the value of an order which, provided the gifts aren't self-branded, frequently find themselves in the draw. We don't bother categorizing into first prize, second prize and so on – the first ticket drawn gets to choose anything from the pool of prizes, the next ticket out gets to choose from whatever is left, and so on. At one Christmas event we wrapped up all of the prizes so it became impossible to see what they were - a real lottery.

We did, on one occasion, try a prize draw. These differ slightly to above in that compliance with licensing authority requirements is needed. If you're going down this route, then we would suggest to discuss with the Licensing Officer in your local Council as documentation on the web can be confusing. For our prize draw we were required to register our "society" (i.e. our Scout Group) via the local Licensing Officer (which required a fee to be paid) and the tickets we sold had to display the date and venue of the prize draw as well as the address of the licensed organizer.

Which to be honest was all a bit of a faff. We'd gone down the prize draw route simply because we'd approached various local businesses which had given us some decent raffle prizes – meals for two, various vouchers, a family cinema ticket and suchlike. We'd thought these to be a bit too good for a humble raffle so we'd printed prize draw tickets ourselves (more aggro – the tickets had to be numbered, stapled into books of five tickets, and run through a sewing-machine to perforate the ticket stubs) and pre-sold them in advance of the draw event (one of our race nights – see further on). Overall we made a few quid but it definitely wasn't worth the trouble of organizing. We reverted to the plain old simple on-the-day raffle for all events from then on irrespective of the value of the prizes.

Christmas Card Post Service

In the spirit of trying new things, one year we organized a postal service for Christmas cards. We know other Scout Groups manage to do this quite successfully so we thought it worth a shot. It involved:

CHRISTMAS CARD
scouts be prepared ... **DELIVERY SERVICE**

Stay in the warm while 17th Reigate Scout Group deliver your Christmas cards to family, friends & neighbours.

Last Christmas!

• RH1 & RH2 post codes
• Post in the special boxes in church
• Last posting date : 19th December

Special scout stamps only 25p each available from church repository.

See reverse for details.

All proceeds to the new scout hall fund

- Advertising it in early November and selling "stamps" for the purchaser to stick onto their Christmas mail. The cost of our "stamps" was about 50% of the prevailing rate for second-class post.
- Putting a "post box" at the back of church, complete with final posting dates
- Sorting the addresses into close-proximity areas for delivery
- Persuading parents to deliver the bundles of post.

The idea was taken up with great enthusiasm by the Parish, and we ended up with about 2,000 cards to deliver - not too bad, we thought, for a first attempt. The pain really started when we had to sort and deliver them. Even though we had restricted our postal area to RH1 and RH2 we hadn't really researched it well enough:

- The postal areas were non-contiguous and relatively large, so sometimes our drivers were travelling miles to deliver a single card
- We had no idea where some of the roads were despite having ex-postmen among our parents
- We couldn't read some of the hand-written addresses
- We couldn't find some of the houses. One address genuinely read "Proceed down xxx road in Woodhatch direction. Take track on left just after the xxx pub. Willie's house is the second on the left". I have blurred two details with xxx just in case by some miracle someone could actually use them to track down Willie's house. We couldn't.

In short, it turned into a nightmare. It did improve our knowledge of the local area but almost certainly cost the drivers more in fuel than the scheme raised. For some of the addresses we simply couldn't find we ended up sticking a conventional stamp on the envelope and entrusting it to the professionals.

We have since found out what's needed to make the scheme work more effectively (more collection points for example, and only one delivery date) but the consensus from all of the drivers was "never again".

A Miscellany of Fairs

We have taken stalls at various local fairs. These have included a Diamond Jubilee Fair, various May fairs, and various Christmas fairs. These again fall into the category of dual-purpose to raise awareness.

Running a stall at these kinds of fair pre-supposes we had something to sell. For most we had a food concession and were cooking burgers and bacon rolls over a catering-sized barbeque and selling them accompanied by the usual array of buns, relishes, fried onions and so on. Sometimes we had asked parents to bake home-made cakes which were always a good seller. For the Christmas fair we usually had an array of hand-crafted decorations and trinkets.

The problems we usually faced were that we seldom had an exclusive concession to sell food, so we were in competition with professional burger vans or other stalls with home-made cakes, and at the Christmas fairs practically every other stall had artisan decorations which meant very discerning customers. Setting up the stalls was also incredibly hard work, especially for the outdoor events. The day would start very early in a morning loading all of the gear into a trailer or van, then pitching a marquee and setting out tables and the stalls. If we were flipping burgers then they had to be collected and kept refrigerated, onions had to be chopped, buckets of ice found for cold drinks, and so it goes on. At the end of the day, when everyone was tired, this process had to be reversed to clear away and almost always we were left with the problem of what to do with the unsold stock.

> **Accidents happen**
>
> Despite the most rigorous risk assessments, injuries occur due to unforeseen circumstances.
>
> We collected a trailer-load of bread-rolls and had secured the trays using bungees, some of which had been stretched a bit tight. When Tony released one of these the other end pinged forward at high velocity, with the hook catching him above his right eye. He was dispatched to A&E, dazed and bloodied, returning a few hours later with a neat row of stitches and a Band-Aid and placed on onion-chopping duties. We don't think any blood made it onto the bread rolls.

Weather also played a part, with rainy or cold conditions reducing attendance and affecting both financial return and our ability to raise awareness. If you get the impression that I wasn't personally a fan of doing these then you'd be right. Despite the good publicity (if it hadn't rained) the man-hours required to organize and execute these events weren't in my opinion, worth the relatively low profit margin.

Race Nights

Our Race Nights have become somewhat legendary, attracting both new audiences and returning families, and provoking fierce competition among those taking part. Some "jockeys" have been known to train before a race to increase the odds of them winning.

We are not talking conventional race nights here, where maybe there is a film shown of a race and punters bet on the outcome. Our race nights are deliciously Scout-ish and all the more popular for being so. The ingredients are very simple. We find a large venue (our new Parish centre has proved fine but we have recently tried a race night in our new Scout Hall which worked very well.) Lanes are laid out on the floor using masking tape, maybe twenty metres long and wide enough for four human jockeys side-by-side. Each jockey has a "horse", which is a cut-out silhouette on a flat wooden base located at the starting end of the track. The "horse" is attached to a long piece of cord which wraps round a hand-powered winder positioned at the winning-line end of the track. When the race starts the "jockey", who is kneeling down behind the winning line, simply has to wind the handle as fast as possible to draw the "horse" over the finish.

What makes it fun is the nuances introduced.

The tote: Before a race starts punters are asked to bet on which "horse" they fancy. At that stage the jockeys have not yet been selected so no-one knows who will be winding which "horse". Though, somewhat irrationally, certain "horses" do attract more bets than others and equally mystifying, one particular "horse" can be far more successful than the others over the course of an evening despite being nominally the same and "ridden" by different jockeys. For the wives' race we deliberately allocate the "horse" to the jockey (i.e. the wife) <u>before</u> opening the tote. There is then a lot of speculation and banter on whether the husband will actually bet on his wife winning.

The "horses":   Double-quotes have been used deliberately when describing the "horses" since there is actually only one horse. We also have a pig, a chicken, and a cow. Last Christmas we raced reindeer. We also got our Scout Section to make some new additions, which led to racing a bicycle, a racing car, a snail, and most notably, a bloke sitting on a toilet. The latter attracted a lot of bets.

The races: A typical race night comprises around ten races. Each race is themed and the names of the horse (or pig/chicken/cow) reflect the theme of the race.

Race 5: Two's Company
(place your bets on)
Horse and Carriage
Cow and Gate
Pig and Whistle
Chicken and Egg
Duck and Dive

Race 6: Doctor's Orders
Feeling hoarse
Foot and mouth
The trots
Chickenpox
Ellie's ears

This can lead to some interesting race commentary: "…'Ellie's ears' are at the back of the field with 'The trots'. 'Chickenpox' is making a late surge but cannot catch 'Foot and mouth' after 'Feeling hoarse'… " But the real fun starts when selecting the jockey for an individual race. We usually try to balance the choice so one does not have an obvious physical advantage over the others, thus we might call for jockeys who are all under six years old, or who are all grandparents (for whom we normally provide chairs for them to sit on and wind), or just from the Scout Section. But testosterone flows and alpha males appear when we ask for dads to be the jockeys. Boy does an innocent game suddenly get competitive and serious.

But not, it has to be said, as competitive or serious as when we hold a "husbands and wives" race. With this race there is a line midway down the course marking the changeover point – when the horse has crossed it then husbands must transfer winding responsibility to their wife (or vice versa depending on who wound first). It gets particularly rowdy at the half-way mark – it has been known for wives to be hurled aside bodily by their husbands in the ferocity to take over the winding as fast as possible.

As an evening's entertainment it's pretty unbeatable – a lot of fun suitable for all ages. We never make tons of money at it, though the tote usually does pretty well and obviously there is a raffle in the mix, but it costs nothing for us to stage and, as we've done it so often, the organization is down to a fine art and takes less than an hour to set up.

Teas and coffees (and cakes and marmalade and bacon sarnies)

Over the past few years we must have served hundreds of mugs of tea and coffee and given away thousands of biscuits, and every month after the family Mass at church we continue to dispense even more. Occasionally we include bacon rolls which never last long. The trick, we have found, is not to set a price but to ask for donations into a bucket. Generally, people cannot believe it when we respond "it's free" to their "how much is a cup

of…" question (especially if a free bacon roll is offered) and almost always more change goes into our bucket than had we charged the prevailing rate. Sometimes we combine our free teas and coffees with a sale of home-made cakes or jars of marmalade, which again proves popular. Our Beavers painted some very colourful "Free tea/coffee after Mass" signs which we position strategically by the exits, and we are never short of customers as a result.

It's also a good opportunity to meet a few of the parents of our Beavers, Cubs and so on, or to catch up with former members, and we normally come away with a few enquiries of "how do we get our son/daughter a place" from newcomers to the Parish. Very occasionally we might recruit another volunteer. Once our Scout Hall was up and running we also gave a few personal guided tours to Parishioners including to several who had donated generously to our cause. This level of interaction would have been difficult without the opportunity created simply by serving a few hot drinks each month.

Section-specific fund-raising

In our quest to involve our young people in the project, we thought it a good idea to set each Section a challenge to raise funds for something specific and permanent. We reasoned this would give their campaigns a focus and, if successful, would enable them to point in the future at something tangible and know that they had contributed to its purchase. Looking through our shopping-list of things still to buy, we wanted to avoid anything likely to wear out or need replacement – so furniture and equipment was ruled out. We settled on asking Sections to find funding for the fire escape. Not the most glamorous of items but it will be there for the lifetime of the building and is part of the intrinsic safety requirements. It also fitted in nicely with the target we had in mind for each Section to raise - £300 over the course of a term.

Our Sections rose to the challenge admirably, with some far exceeding the target, and all met the challenge in different and imaginative ways.

- Our Beaver Section held a disco for which admission was charged and drinks and sweets sold. Our Explorers ran the disco, strengthening cross-Section cooperation.

- Our Cub Leaders (and some Cubs) undertook a mud-run which, having seen some of the photos, lived up to its name. The Leaders sought sponsorship from far and wide which ensured the target was reached easily.

- Our Scouts took up an opportunity from a newly-established local business, whose owner was seeking a group to deliver leaflets to houses in a particular catchment. The slight snag was that he asked for 15,000 leaflets to be delivered which far exceeded the number of houses available. I think in the end around half that number were delivered but our Scout Section found it hard going as enthusiasm waned and it took much longer that they had planned. As it was seen to be for a good cause, the original amount pledged was honoured and thus the target was met.

- Our Explorers ran a quiz evening, which was well-attended even if there was a certain degree of contention from some teams about a few of the answers. Google to the rescue for the organizers. Good fun though and that, together with a later book sale, meant they reached the goal for their Section.

As an approach to fund-raising this worked well and would be repeatable, though probably not that often.

Santa Walks

Since seemingly forever, each December our Scout Group has supported the local Round Table in collecting money door-to-door for its good causes. This involves Santa's Sleigh (actually a car towing a fairly old caravan with Santa sticking his head out of a faux chimney) driving slowly around a set route of streets, with Santa encouraging children to come outside ("come to your windows, come to your doors, come and say hi to Santa Claus") whilst a posse of volunteers (i.e. 17th Reigate) knocks on doors shaking Round Table collection tins. The caravan is playing a selection of Christmas hits, very loudly to attract attention. This continues throughout most of the month to ensure that the town gets covered, and 17th Reigate does two or three of the routes in exchange for a fixed donation from the Round Table.

For some inexplicable reason this is hugely popular with our young people. For me (and other curmudgeonly "oldies"), listening to endless loud and tinny renditions of George Michael lamenting over and over about the recipient of his heart then giving it away blah blah blah is enough to renew annual membership of the bah-humbug club. But whenever we publish the rota for our Christmas fund-raising activities, the Santa Walks are booked up first and they are almost always oversubscribed. Not that there is a limit, but we reckon about twenty kids knocking on doors is a manageable number. One year we had over eighty children and parents following Santa. Out of curiosity I timed from when the caravan passed me to when the last person had gone past. It took over twenty minutes and looked like a surreal version of the Pied Piper. For the children at the front it becomes a bit of a competition to knock on the next door, which is why around twenty kids is ideal – everyone will get a turn. When we had eighty, the ones at the back were re-knocking on doors already knocked, to the irritation of parents opening the door for a second time.

Obviously there are health and safety requirements which we have to address. All of the young people have to wear high visibility waistcoats; we have some adults at the front by the caravan and others at the back sweeping up stragglers. No child is allowed to go inside a house or knock on a door on their own – they must be in pairs, and everything stops at around 9pm irrespective of whether all streets on the particular route have been covered. There's a soup-stop midway to restore energy levels and on occasion, thaw out.

This is another event which gets our young people interacting with the public, and from that viewpoint it is very worthwhile doing. When money is put into their collecting tins we try to encourage the kids to say "Happy Christmas" and "thank you" and not to make it sound too much like a threat. We nearly came unstuck one year when one of our Cubs (Tom of special-needs pizza-rustling fame from bag-packing) was greeted by a very pregnant lady at a door. Tom politely thanked her for her donation as we had coached, adding at the end "You're really fat. Why're you fat?". We whisked him away sharpish before anyone started to explain.

As an event it's firmly established in our calendar – we never know which routes we will be offered but we know that the offer will always be made and for the kids at least, it's fun.

Carol-singing

Much of our fund-raising occurs in the run-up to Christmas, and the smorgasbord of events has included, for the last two or three years, singing carols at innocent commuters as they leave Redhill station. As an event it needs little explanation. A merry band of our mainly-conscripted young people wearing Scout scarves and seasonal hats, with a few brave leaders and even braver parents, congregate on the station concourse and, well, sing carols. Occasionally we have had a few musical instruments joining in, but mostly it's just singing, with strategically placed buckets for donations.

We're honestly not sure what commuters make of it although they are very generous maybe through excess Christmas spirit or perhaps just pity: in the couple of hours when we do it we always make far more than I feel we ought and the run-rate is not far off that from bag-packing. We suspect some of the donations are almost given as protection money: in the lull between train arrivals then often a single commuter has to run the gauntlet of passing twenty or thirty singers at full volume giving him or her their full attention. If they are not expecting it this can be somewhat intimidating.

Friends of the 17th

As if building a new Scout Hall was not sufficient, 2015 also saw the start of the Group's centenary year. Various celebrations were planned; a birthday party, Section events to mark the occasion, and a Centenary camp over one of the May Bank Holidays (including our challenge to cook 100 pancakes in 100 minutes – successfully achieved and consumed in a considerably shorter period). Although the camp would be for current members only, we wanted to reach some of our past members and invite them to the camp-fire. This would be an opportunity for them to re-live some of their Scouting days, meet friends with whom they may have lost contact, and see how the Group had thrived in the intervening period. Somewhat cynically, it would also mean we had a captive audience for a few hours to explain all about our "Building For The Future" project and on the back of a feel-good factor from toasting marshmallows again around the camp-fire, maybe we could coax a few quid from them.

These days, with social media and the multitude of ways in which people can stay in touch, finding a way of contacting friends is pretty straightforward even for those with whom contact has been lost. But reaching people who have been out of contact for ten years or more is far more difficult. We had no database of details – Data Protection had seen to that – so therein lay our challenge. We created this concept of "Friends of the 17th" – a kind of alumni for former members. We had a nice flyer prepared about our centenary celebrations and inviting them to become an "honorary Scout" for a term or year, in exchange for a suggested donation. We culled names of past members from the Group archives and added more after the "old timers" in the Group had examined loads of old photos (prompting evening-long distractions down memory lane... "that's such and such. Do you remember when...").

So we had marketing material, and a list of a few hundred recipients. The problem we never came close to solving was how to get in touch with them. For a handful we had email addresses. A few more were reached via friends-of-friends. But the majority remained unreachable and with that "Friends of the 17th" gently faded away and (both of) our honorary Scouts who had signed up were kind enough not to keep reminding us about it. The few we did manage to contact were invited to our birthday party and the camp-fire and both events were great social successes. But as a fund-raiser it hadn't worked.

Children's Disco

Another event we tried also wasn't the success we'd hoped for, although this may have been due to timing rather than the idea itself. One year, in that awkward period between Christmas and New Year, we ran a children's disco. Or rather two discos – one on a Saturday afternoon for younger children, and one in the evening for the older kids. The idea was that it would give the kids something to do for a couple of hours and thus their parents some respite. This involved very little capital outlay as we had all of the disco sound equipment and lighting – all we had to purchase was a few drinks and sweets which would be sold.

This kind of event requires a critical mass of attendees to generate a lively atmosphere and to have a hope of success. The afternoon disco just about achieved that and we were able to intersperse the music with silly games and the like – very popular with the thirty or so 6-10 year-olds who were there. For the evening disco, we had four young people there. Or maybe five. Whatever the number it wasn't many and after dancing to a couple of songs they had resorted to standing awkwardly around the fringes of the room in the certain knowledge that they were it – no-one else would be joining them. We knocked it on the head after twenty minutes, refunded the entry money, and packed up early.

Scavenging materials

Not strictly fund-raising but scavenging materials which could be used in the build saved us thousands of pounds and so I felt it worthy of inclusion in this section. I mentioned before that some of us have a certain reputation as skip-raiders, finding it very difficult to pass one by without glancing inside it to see if there's anything which could be useful. With this project we elevated the practice of scavenging to new levels. Here is a précis of what we scrounged:

Flooring

Not to be outdone by the new Parish Centre at St. Joseph's church, its sister church in Reigate decided it too wanted a new church hall. In an almost identical scenario, the existing church hall would be demolished, the land sold, and the proceeds used to build the new hall. As luck would have it the hall to be demolished was not far off the area of footprint of our new Scout Hall. Inside it was this wooden flooring – lovely age-patinated solid oak tongue-and-grooved planks laid over thin sleepers. With a surface area which would cover around three quarters of the floor in our first-floor main hall.

Negotiations ensued with the demolition company who, with some gentle encouragement from the Parish Development Committee, allowed us to take all of the flooring for free provided we lifted it ourselves and did so before demolition was due to start. We also had to get an asbestos survey done on the substrate beneath the floor to mitigate any health risks from disturbing the surface. Prudent, as the hall had been built when asbestos was all the rage and was being added into anything, including solid concrete bases.

One baking hot July morning an army of volunteers descended on the Holy Family church hall and stripped the floor bare in about four hours. Around 150 square metres of oak flooring was prised up carefully to preserve the tongue and groove, and de-nailed. We estimated that around four tonnes of flooring was lifted and around 10,000 nails were removed that day. The hot work didn't end with the removal of the flooring, for now we had to load it, transport it, and offload it. Thus began the first of eventually six moves of four tonnes of oak flooring.

Move One was from the hall to a lock-up garage loaned to us by a local housing association. Unloading it took ages – all of the oak planks were different lengths and thus had to be stacked like a form of horizontal Tetris to stop the boards from warping. Two months later we discovered that the roof leaked quite badly and despite tarpaulins, the flooring was starting to suffer. Another plea for volunteers for Move Two – from the lock-up to a disused training centre loaned to us at the local aerodrome. More Tetris, more splinters. Then there was a fire in the café at the aerodrome, which meant our training centre was required by paying guests, however the aerodrome management found us alternative accommodation. Move Three involved moving all of the flooring about seventy metres to a different building. Move Four eventually relocated it, along with all of our Scouting equipment, from the aerodrome to one of the garages now reinstated under our Scout Hall. Move Five was by a workforce from a local company volunteering to help a community project and, in exchange for beer and a barbeque, lifted the flooring from the garage to the first floor hall. Move Six relocated it to the far end of the hall where it wouldn't be in the way. By this time the Tetris system had gone out of the window.

The efforts were worthwhile. To purchase this amount of new flooring would have cost thousands of pounds. Some observations on laying it back down are included in Chapter 5 – Getting It Built but suffice to say, the floor looks fantastic and with its patina of thirty years of use, looks like it has been down for ever.

Industrial racking

As a flourishing Scout Group we have tons of equipment. Tents, marquees, tables, ropes, benches, urns, games, cooking equipment… boxes and boxes of gear. So much stuff, in fact, that we have never had the space to store it properly in such a way that it's obvious what we have and can get to it easily. We've often needed to buy new on the basis we could not find what we knew we had somewhere. One of the design goals of our new Scout Hall was to change this and to give ourselves enough space with some decent easily-accessible shelving.

We heard of a factory closing down which had a warehouse facility and they were proposing to scrap all of the industrial racking since its resale value was minimal. For the cost of a bottle of sloe gin for the facilities manager, and the hire of a 7.5-tonne van to collect it, we got the lot for free – around sixty linear metres of three-bay five-metre high industrial racking.

Yet more industrial racking (and yet more flooring)

Another office was closing down and we were invited to help ourselves from their store which had been used for computer equipment. An evening working-party descended, unbolted miles of lightweight racking, and loaded it into a transit van. Even better, the flooring in the store comprised interlocking hard rubber tiles, so we had all of that away as well – around 100 square metres – and later laid it in our Scout store. In fact, our magpies were especially busy that evening for there was a ton of ex-IT equipment left behind and we came away with boxes of cabling, power rails, an old phone system (boxed as new), and some step-ladders. We would have had more but by then the suspension on the transit van was in danger of collapse.

Hoardings

We knew we would need a lot of 18mm ply to board out the first floor and also as a structural surface under the zinc roof. We also knew that there were a lot of building sites around the area whose hoardings comprised... 18mm ply. We found out that the majority of this goes into landfill after a building has been completed and this, we thought, was our opportunity. We could offer to take it off the developers' hands, save them the disposal cost, and save ourselves a fortune by re-purposing it into flooring.

A few gentle enquiries later with the main contractors on a few of these sites and some fortuitous timing to get in as the hoardings were coming down meant we got about forty sheets of 2.4m x 1.2m exterior-grade ply completely free. Some of it had been painted and some of the edges were a bit ragged but for what we wanted it was ideal. The contractors were very pleased too, supporting a local good cause.

Office furniture

Another office was closing, this time due to re-location to new premises which came complete with posh furniture. All of their old furniture was thus up for grabs. Another evening, another salvage crew, another Luton van and we came away with numerous cupboards, two-drawer and four-drawer filing-cabinets, three clocks, and two anglepoise lamps (the magpie instinct kicking in again). All of the furniture has been used as storage in our meeting room and hall.

Lighting

Not so much scavenged as donated, we were given a stack of industrial fluorescent lighting battens of different types and some emergency lighting. Although we used LED lighting in our main hall and meeting room, we used these donated fittings for all lighting elsewhere. The same source donated our fire detection system – a modern addressable alarm panel and all of the sensors.

Paint

A local decorating shop offered us what they described as "a few tins of mis-tints or customer-unwanted paint". Without exaggeration we collected in excess of three hundred tins of every size and paint type imaginable: emulsion, gloss, primer, metal, specialist, tester pots, fence preserver… you name it, and in almost every colour imaginable. Way more than we could possibly use as the opportunity for colour was limited – our primary colour scheme is white though we did paint some cupboards and walls in feature colours from among the tins, not that this made much impact on the amount. The surplus was delivered to our local technical college for use by their painting and decorating apprentices.

Mahogany

I mentioned early on that the old church hall at St. Joseph's was equipped with a bar. The bar itself was made from mahogany which in turn had been salvaged from the adjacent former school library and science labs which had been demolished when the church was built. The mahogany had a long connection with the Parish and was part of our history – justification for Tony and me nipping into the building one afternoon and salvaging all of it ahead of the building's demolition. A case, if I recall, of act first and apologize afterwards if required.

There is now a feature wall in the new Scout Hall made from the mahogany, on which is mounted a Pascal Lamb plaque also salvaged from the old school. The "Board of Fame" in our lobby which acknowledges our sponsors and donors is also made from the mahogany, preserving the historic connection with the Parish and what has gone before.

An old sink

The local municipal sports centre was re-fitting its kitchens and had left outside the old sink and work surface, both free-standing and made of stainless steel. These were appropriated one dark night and after months of storage and moving (and re-moving à la oak flooring), came in useful. The work surface was cut down using an angle grinder (VERY NOISY) to form the counter-top by our serving hatch from the kitchen and the sink was donated to the local District camp-site and very pleased they were with it.

Skip-raiding (and reverse skip-raiding)

Ironically, we salvaged little from skips themselves. David spotted some fibreglass insulation which was retrieved and used to plug some gaps in floorboards but that was pretty much it. Clearly we weren't the only ones in the game either; having chucked a load of scrap metal into our skip on site it had disappeared the next day into the back of the local scrap wagon doing its rounds. Poetic reverse skip-raiding, I suppose.

Our scavenging instinct saved the project thousands of pounds. Just as importantly it showed that by taking advantage of opportunities for utilizing items otherwise regarded as waste, there is a clear and demonstrable message to our young people over the value of recycling.

House-clearance

This was one of the most bizarre ways in which we raised funds. We were approached by the brother of a recently-deceased gentleman who had lived locally. He was seeking assistance in emptying the contents of his brother's house in exchange for a donation and any of the contents which we wanted to take. Being a former Scout himself but now living abroad, he wanted to pass the opportunity to a local Scout Group.

A recce showed that maybe the task wasn't quite as straightforward as might have been imagined. The deceased gentleman had been rather a hoarder. Or to be precise, he had kept every copy of the Times and Sunday Times (complete with supplements) published in the last fifty years. These were in piles in every room all over the house. Some were tied up in bundles, most were loose. Many of the local freebie papers were in the mix too. Nonetheless we sensed an opportunity since we knew that within the last fifty years there must be those editions more valuable because they marked a significant event – the moon landing, royal weddings, state funerals and the like. Also editions for people wanting to mark their own significant anniversaries. We uncovered our first problem – none of the newspapers were stacked in chronological order. Fifty years of newspapers is nigh on 20,000 editions and the thought of searching for specific ones was not an appealing one.

The second problem was moving them.   20,000 newspapers weigh tons – literally. And these were very dusty.

We got round the second problem over a couple of weekends with another army of volunteers chain-ganging bundles of papers out of the house into vans and trailers then driven to a dry garage for temporary storage. Dust-masks were essential as was a long hot shower afterwards. We also salvaged a few other bits and pieces. Most of the contents other than the newspapers had already gone to family members so there was little remaining of any value for us. There was however a drinks cabinet stocked with various Sherries and ports, some of quite elderly vintage. These were dusted off and appeared as raffle prizes over subsequent months.

The first problem – what to do with all of the newspapers – was solved by David in a typically innovative way. He contacted the handful of UK companies which sell vintage newspapers and offered all of ours for free provided they collected them. In return, if any turned out to be valuable then maybe they would consider a donation to our cause. Most were not interested but one company did take them off our hands. The owner was rather disgruntled to later discover that not only was the old boy a hoarder but also he had been an inveterate crossword addict – most puzzles had been completed and there were anagrams and doodling all over the margins of the back pages. This effectively prevented any of the papers from being sold in mint condition and thus devalued them considerably – not really what he wanted to find having driven from Cornwall to collect them.

There was a footnote to this story in that when we did the second clearance party, the brother who had engaged us pointed out an old garage in which he said there was a car – he didn't know what state it was in but again, ours if we wanted it – one less problem for him to deal with. Briefly, there was great excitement. Could be a vintage motor, we speculated, maybe even veteran given the somewhat eccentric nature of its owner. Then we wrestled opened the garage doors and saw…an old beige Austin Maxi. Flat tyres, rotting windscreen rubbers, rust showing through – it was in a very sorry state. We had no chance of getting it out of the garage - vintage indeed but not quite what we hoped for. David's lateral thinking to the rescue once more: as there are collectors' clubs for almost everything these days, he found one for Austin Maxis and a member there bought it for spares. We had briefly entered the used-car market and came away a couple of hundred quid up.

Tuck Shop

There have been flashes of entrepreneurial spirit among both young people and Leaders.

One of our Explorers regularly sets up a tuck shop at camps and social events which proves especially popular with the younger age-ranges. Sourcing sweets and drinks from the local wholesaler he regularly returns a profit of £20-£30 each time. And one summer a Cub/Scout brother/sister team made dozens of paracord bracelets which were sold to friends and family and also at some of our craft fairs. All of these ideas came from themselves and it was entirely fitting that they received "Above and Beyond" awards presented at one of our AGMs.

On a similar theme one of our Leaders sells drinks and snacks to his co-workers and gives us a bag of change every few months. We loaned him one of the camp fridges so he could offer cold drinks in the summer, increasing the sales still further.

Christmas Craft Morning

We tried this for the first time last Christmas. We bought a load of Christmas decorations, glitter, glue, stencils, icing, cake decorations and so on and invited kids to come along for a couple of hours and make Christmas themed goodies, either decorative or edible. The idea was pitched to enable mum and dad to go off and do a bit of Christmas shopping whilst able to leave their offspring in a safe environment with, for a nominal entrance fee, things for them to do and make.

The attendance wasn't brilliant – we think we timed it a bit too early in December and maybe we hadn't advertised it as thoroughly as we might. Also there were competing events locally. But, we broke even and had bought enough materials for the next few years as well, thus ensuring that when we run it again then it will be profitable.

Crowd-funding

Without a doubt this was our least-successful venture. Crowd-funding has the potential to be very profitable though generally it needs a product or concept (to give investors the prospect of a reward) or suitable cause (around which investors can rally). And it needs a route to market – maybe through one of the many crowd-funding websites available.

We thought we had what was needed to make it a success. We had a good cause (our "Building For The Future" project) and a ready route to market (a social media website aimed at Scouting globally with a user-group of tens of thousands). Thus we launched, via an impassioned plea to the user group, a request for funding. After one month we had raised the princely sum of £12.

Looking at why this hadn't worked it seemed we had fallen into a number of traps.

- We had used a social media group for a purpose which wasn't its intent – one or two people objected and caused negative feedback
- A message to a user-group only stays obviously visible until others post more recent messages. Then the older ones scroll down the screen, out of sight and out of mind.
- The "hook" wasn't especially strong – kind of 'please give us some money for a project which, though laudable, will give you absolutely no return'.
- The campaign was static – a "fire and forget" message without any content refresh or status updates. Talking with people who have made crowd-funding work successfully, the best campaigns are constantly

out there in the faces of their target audiences, re-inventing themselves, difficult to avoid, and shouting about how well they are doing.

Cookie Challenge

One for the summer holidays, we thought. Not dissimilar to the "Bake for Sport Relief" idea, we set all of our Sections the challenge, over a summer break, to bake a bunch of cookies and sell them to friends and families. We provided (tested) recipe ideas and ideas of how to sell and how much to charge.

In hindsight our timing might have been off – we'd have done better to try this early on in the project rather than almost last thing, and we think fundraising fatigue had well and truly set in by then. Some of our young persons stepped up to the challenge and baked and sold far more cookies than we'd asked them to. Most didn't though, and overall the results were quite disappointing.

Donations

From time to time we received donations – some modest, some more substantial, but all most welcome. Many were unsolicited and followed various publicity initiatives, for example status updates to the Parish.

Only once did we actually solicit donations from our base of parents. At the end of the project we had, in effect, run out of money and there were a couple of largish bills to settle. We explained this to parents and asked them if they would consider either a short-term loan to the Group or a donation. Being the stars that they are, some of our parents stepped up and either loaned or donated enough to easily cover the immediate debts. The quid pro quo was one or two wanted to better understand the project finances which we were happy to do via an open meeting.

We have also received a steady trickle of donations via David's public speaking. At one time David held the world record for being the youngest person to sail the Atlantic solo. He is regularly invited to speak at business lunches on his experiences and how these motivated him to succeed in his business life. He's happy to do these talks for free but always at the end would explain about his other full-time job (building a Scout Hall) and hold out his hat for donations to our cause. If the lunch had been particularly bibulous then the donations could be quite generous.

Mile of Pennies

I'll finish the fund-raising stories with one of the best ones we did. As with all of the good ones it started with a simple idea and grew into something quite special. I had read in the newsletter of a Parish in the Midlands about how their church had raised funds by getting parishioners to collect the equivalent of a mile of pennies. Or 79,200 coins to be precise. This, I thought, would be a good one to have ticking away in the background and when complete would have added nearly £800 to the coffers. But... others on our fund-raising team had broader imaginations.

17TH REIGATE (ST. JOSEPH'S) SCOUT GROUP

We are collecting A Mile Of Pennies (and will also try to break a world record)
By September we want to collect one mile of one-penny coins and lay them out in record-breaking time!

This equals 79,200 coins which will weigh over 280Kg and will need to be laid out in under 2 hours and 16 minutes.

And will add almost £800 to our Building For The Future project, fund-raising to provide our own Scout Hall for the first time in our history.

How you can help us!

Our Beavers, Cubs, Scouts, and Explorers would be grateful to receive any spare one-penny coins lying around, or in pockets, or down the back of the sofa, or from wherever!

For more information on our Building For The Future project, please visit our website www.17threigate.org

Having collected the coins, what if (those words again) we then actually laid them out in a line a mile long? And, what if at the same time we had a crack at the world record for doing so.

So, in February 2013 17th Reigate's attempt on the Mile of Pennies world record was launched. Collecting the coins was the easy part. It worked out to around £6 for every child in the Group, to be collected over about six months. We had various checkpoints on the way to make sure we were on target, and a three-line whip towards the end to get us past the £800-mark. We decided early on that anyone who had collected pennies would be entitled to be part of the coin-laying team on the day of the record attempt. We felt this was particularly important as we wanted to make this a really Group-wide activity – one which everyone could participate in irrespective of age or ability.

A few logistical arrangements were required. Finding an indoor venue was paramount, which required us to calculate how much floor area we needed. Gordon, one of our Explorer leaders, armed himself with tape measure and clipboard and found we could just fit into the assembly hall of the local secondary school, who then very generously loaned us the facility for free.

We needed to understand the requirements of the world record, to ensure that validation and technique would both comply. Numerous emails were exchanged with Guinness World Records (GWR), who were very helpful and agreed that we could self-validate provided we had independent scrutineers.

We had to ensure we had a mile of coins. The easiest way was to sort them into bags of £1, weigh each bag, then count the number of bags. Bagging the coins was easy, bagging them accurately less so. We found the most accurate set of kitchen scales we could, weighed each bag, and became adept at knowing whether a bag was one or two pence over or under. Sometimes we couldn't get the weight right and it usually transpired that a foreign coin or two had been snuck in.

We had to figure out how to position the coins along the route. We solved this quite simply in the end by laying down a mile of 20mm masking tape donated by our local decorating store – the coins would be placed on top of the tape ensuring they were laid in a straight line and each touched its neighbour – the latter a stipulation of the record.

We also needed to perfect our coin-laying technique. This involved many evenings of trial and error. Was it better to pick up the coins individually and place them down, or pour out a quid's-worth on the floor and sort of slide them into position? We tried mechanical assistance – a kind of scissor arrangement of two hinged pieces of wood which would trap the coins then joggle them into position. It worked but was deemed illegal by GWR. In the end we came up with a scatter-and-slide technique which was reasonably fast and we got each Section to practise a few times before the big day.

The world record stood, at the time, at 2 hours and 16 minutes. On the day itself we'd arranged for the record to be attempted in the afternoon – just as well for laying down a mile of masking tape took ages and had to be independently verified by a local surveyor with a laser tape measure. We also had to weigh out all of the coins into polystyrene pots and place them into a parc fermé situation to make sure no coins were removed (or added). As an aside, after the event all of these coins – over a quarter-tonne – had to be re-bagged, taken to the bank and re-weighed before they could be paid into our account. This was not a popular task.

Photograph © Neil Jones

When the countdown completed and the time-clock started there was a great atmosphere – a real team spirit among everyone involved. We had teams who self-organized into coin distribution, checking coins touched, supporters, progress-monitors and reporters, laying-rate calculators (were we on track?), and so on.

As a bonding experience for the Group it was unrivalled – Sections, Leaders, and parents came together as one. We let the Beavers lay coins first, then the rest of the Sections followed in order. As "layers" were restricted to a maximum of eight people at any one time then there was constant change as floor and coins took their toll on knees and fingers. Leaders too got involved – that alpha-male (or -female) thing once more as one competed to get their pot of coins down faster than their neighbour. We even had one of our local Councillors helping out. There's a time-lapse video on our website where the day of preparation and coin-laying is reduced to five minutes, and we received great publicity in the local press and also in the national Scouting magazine.

In the end we missed the world record by 16 minutes. Which was a bit disappointing but the event had met most of its objectives:

- It has raised some money
- It had bonded the Group like nothing else
- It had given us a lot of laughs
- It had put the fun firmly in fund-raising

Ideas which fell by the wayside.

Listed below are some of the other ideas the fund-raising committee came up with which usually didn't make it past the drawing board. They've been included in case they inspire others to take them forward or can think of ways to make them work profitably.

3 hills challenge
Sponsored sky-dive
Overnight hike
Endurance event
Hair shave

We contemplated a number of sponsored events, and these were some of them. The theory was to come up with events which for a minimum effort would generate a relatively good return from different audiences. The sponsored sky-dive and some form of endurance event would, we thought, appeal to some sporty mums and dads taking them out of their comfort zone and opening up sponsorship opportunities beyond their immediate families.

The 3 hills challenge fell by the wayside due to logistics – wanting it to be something for the entire Group then it was difficult to resolve a route and timings that would be suitable for both Beavers and Explorers.

It's worth pointing out there was no enthusiasm for the hair-shaving idea.

Celebrity drawings, autographs

This was a variation on asking famous people to donate things for auction. It was inspired by a similar scheme by the Eden Project in 2012 which asked for well-known faces in entertainment, politics, business and so forth to draw a simple picture of anything they liked, which would then be auctioned.

Our twist would be to ask famous ex-Scouts for a drawing, maybe but not necessarily Scouting-related. We would provide two bits of paper – one for their drawing which would be auctioned, and one for an autograph which would be bound into a book and also auctioned.

Identifying ex-Scouts was quite easy – Gilwell holds a list and a web search reveals many more. It's quite an impressive list too, comprising current and former industry leaders, astronauts, politicians, entertainers, nobility and others. We also felt that it wasn't necessary to restrict to just the UK – Scouting is global after all. Locating contact details for these people is actually easier than expected for many of them are still in the public eye.

I'm not entirely sure why we didn't pursue this other than a question of timing and the suspicion that if the Eden Project had inspired us to copy then maybe it had inspired others too. Maybe also there's a limit to a celebrity's pro bono artistic skills.

Do Me A Favour

Another auction variation, this time around an auction of promises. We came up with a long list of things which people might find useful – favours which could be called in - for example

- Make a celebration cake
- Do four hours of babysitting
- Sew on school name tags
- Jet-wash a patio

Calling on the talents and expertise of our parents we proposed to find willing volunteers to do each of these, then auction the favour to the highest bidder, calling it in in the next three months (thus allowing us to do it again).

The difficulty with this idea was finding the willing volunteers to do each of the tasks and in the end the commitment wasn't there. Pity really since I'd have paid to have my patio jet-washed.

Events at which we can sell water

Based in the South East we have a number of sporting events in our area. For example, the London to Brighton cycle ride, many other cycling events inspired by the 2012 Olympics, an annual half-marathon, the Old Crocks race and so on.

One idea was to sell water to competitors and spectators at strategic points along the route of these events (although being in November, hot chocolate was discussed instead of water for the Old Crocks race).

There were some obstacles, including competition, official rest-stops, permissions needed for street trading, and logistics of replenishing stocks of bottled water. Also the weather: we knew from our summer fair experience that on a hot day we could sell loads of cold drinks, but if it rained then no-one was very interested.

The 20 500 club

Here we thought about identifying twenty local companies who would be willing to each donate £500 towards our project. In return they would have a number of hours of exclusive use of the new facilities for meetings, conferences and suchlike.

The problem with this idea was finding the right contact in enough local companies – the person who could make a decision. There are mailing lists which can be bought but for this they would be relatively expensive. Working on a 5% success rate meant we would have to identify 1000 local businesses and write to all of them – expensive in postage, printing, and time needed.

Swear-box

We would have made a small fortune had we introduced a swear-box at the start of the project, and the income from fines on the day of the hall opening alone would have reduced the Group's debt considerably.

It is fair to say that there was a direct correlation between stress as the big day approached and the fruitiness of language on site. Particularly profitable would have been the time when David dropped his brand-new tape-measure into a very muddy puddle. Well, the rest of us thought it funny.

In conclusion, what did we learn?

Keep it simple

Simple ideas work best - true for many things and fund-raising is no different. The more complicated an idea, the more difficult the logistics, the more difficult it becomes to rally support, and most likely, a lower rate of return.

Variety is good

Mixing up different types of events keeps the fund-raising initiative alive and feeling fresh. There's nothing wrong in trying out new ideas – some of course won't work but others will work better than imagined and open themselves up for re-use. Introducing new members to a fund-raising committee also helps to spark innovation and involvement.

Successes can be re-used

Generally, it's apparent without a lot of analysis which ideas work well and can be repeated. Caution should be exercised about the frequency of repetition but a good fund-raising plan has a balance of new ideas which need to be tested and old favourites guaranteed to bring in some money.

Avoid clashes

After some near-misses we got into the habit of checking if other events were planned for the same dates as our fund-raising. Particularly in the Parish and the local schools, and especially in the run-up to Christmas.

Introduce fun

Putting the fun into fund-raising may sound a bit corny, but the more fun an event is to stage then the better response from children, parents, and organizers. Our Mile of Pennies challenge is a case in point – although it didn't raise a massive amount it was great fun to stage and brought the Group together.

It takes hard work!

No fund-raising is easy. The basic principle of trying to extract money from people for a cause which may not directly relate to them requires bucket-loads of commitment and tenacity. Big events require more organization before, during, and afterwards and an inordinate amount of time often needs to be invested in even the simplest of schemes.

Charity fatigue is real

It's pretty essential to target different audiences and markets and avoid tapping up the same people for money time after time. Otherwise, they eventually get cross and switch off, not only from the immediate request but future ones too.

This might seem blatantly obvious but in reality there's a strong temptation to go after the same people who have supported a cause before.

It's not all about money

In pure finance terms, the effort versus return ratio for many of our events was not great, to the point where common sense suggested not to proceed with or repeat the event. But, we knew from the start that we were not only seeking to raise money but also seeking to raise awareness and support for the project in general. We knew this would become important both when we started to build the hall and also afterwards when we wanted to expand the Group. So the socials we ran, for example, provided a way of bringing the community together and getting behind us. This was as valuable to us as hard cash.

The original block of garages and stores, replaced with our new Scout Hall

Listening for activity in the unexpectedly-discovered sewer-pipe

Even snow didn't stop construction

Fr. Chris lays the first brick

Scout TV at 35,000 feet on route to Copenhagen

The start of an awful lot of painting

Age was no barrier to helping

Our regular audience. Now entombed in the walls, forever watching...

So, how many does it really take to put up a sheet of plasterboard?

All hail the angle-grinder

Celebrating laying the first metre of oak flooring

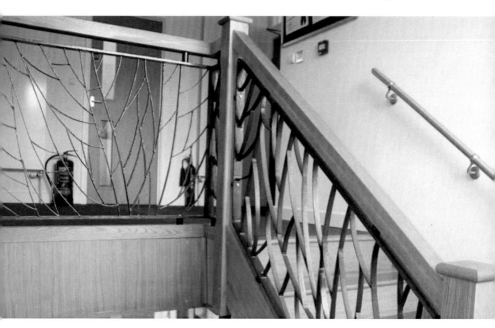

Our custom-made balustrades

Photograph ©Neil Jones

Her Worshipful the Mayor of the Borough of Reigate and Banstead opens the building

View down the main hall

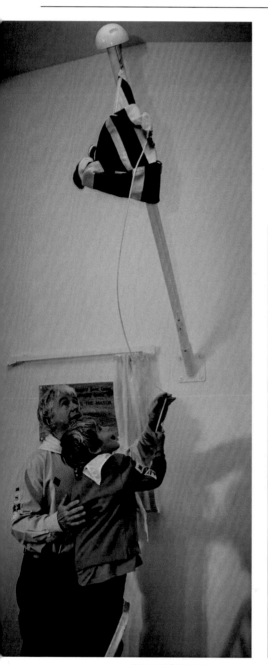

Photograph ©Neil Jones

The first flag-break. Now it's a
proper Scout Hall

Inauguration of the climbing wall
Photograph ©Neil Jones

4 – OUR APPROACH TO THE ART OF GRANT APPLICATION

Lots of books have been written and seminars held on the art of writing funding applications. In no way do we want to muscle in on this territory as their authors are much more skilled and experienced than us. What is written below is how <u>we</u> approached the task – as an art form definitely more playgroup than Picasso. No doubt professional funding application writers and advisers will despair at the way we fumbled towards our results though in our defence we achieved a success-rate of around 12%, apparently better than the average return. In our naivety we saw the process as:

1) Find the funders (research)
2) Ask them nicely for money
3) Expect the cheque, naturally by return mail
4) Write them a letter of thanks
5) Try and avoid asking them again
6) Communicate progress

Amazingly this is pretty close to what we actually did (though we had a reality check in step 3 - definitely not cheque by return mail) but there were nuances and refinements along the way which increased the success factor.

Step 1) Find the funders

It's worth stressing that researching funders was not a one-off exercise: our quest for financial backing continued throughout the project lifetime and at least one-third of our funding came from funders not identified in our initial research.

I have already mentioned Funding Central - the free-to-access Government-backed database of funding sources - as being an extremely effective way of locating donors. The box below shows the criteria we set up which yielded around 600 results. As well as one-off searches, Funding Central will email a weekly digest of funders matching the defined search criteria which have approaching deadlines for applications.

<u>Our search criteria</u>

What kind of organisation do you represent?

Registered charity, Voluntary and community organisation

How would you describe what you do?

Promoting community cohesion, Promoting education and learning, Promoting religion and religious activity, Promoting volunteering, Supporting sport and recreational activities, Working with people with disabilities, Working with young people

How would you describe your main activity?

Arts and cultural activities, Equipment, Events and workshops, General community benefit, Organised sport and activities, Promoting equal opportunities, Regular meetings, Skills development, Training

What do you want the funding for?

Alterations to buildings or land

Who will benefit from your work?

Volunteers, Agnostic/Atheist/No religion, Buddhism, Christianity, Hinduism, Islam, Judaism, Other, Sikhism, Groups, Children (1-11), Young people (12-18), Young adults (19-25), Adults (26-60), Female, Male, Asian, Black, Chinese, Mixed, Other, White

---

Following the coarse sieving process described on page 15, we were left with around 100 possibilities which needed further follow-up. The approach thereafter was to Google each name to find out additional information. Often this would be the Charity Commission entry which sometimes gave slightly more information on the aims of the charity, but most significantly gave contact details. One or more of three actions then followed:

- Research on the organization's website
- Phone call
- Letter (or email) of introduction

The organization's website

Most large funders have a website, within which the application process and, more valuably, the criteria for awarding a grant (and often, what <u>won't</u> be funded), are usually set out. There may also be case-studies or lists of previous awards. This information usually allowed a much better judgement to be made of the chances of success. And it pays to read this carefully – I once wasted a day completing an application form for a grant from Comic Relief only to find out that capital building projects were not supported. This was pretty clearly stated in the list of exclusions on their website.

The phone call

Where there was no additional information available (and often even where there was), we adopted the approach of phoning the contact name in the organization. This was pretty daunting to start with and akin to being a call-centre operator touting for mis-sold PPI business. However, it got easier the more we did it and saved a lot of wasted effort in making unsuitable applications. The phone-call normally went along the lines of

- Explaining who we were (a uniformed Scout Group located in the South East)
- Explaining the nature of the project (a capital build project)
- Asking if this was the kind of project which they would consider supporting

Most were quick calls and consequently we discounted over half of the remaining organizations on the basis that we did not qualify. Interestingly the majority of disqualifications were due to geography, where we were outside the territory supported by the organization. With many organizations listing their charitable aims as simply "general charitable activities" this would have been impossible to spot without a phone call to clarify. We did learn to recognize Scottish charities as their charity number starts with SC – these we moved to our "Not a Chance" category, reasoning that the South East of England is a long way from the Scottish border and they would have no shortage of suitable causes much closer to home.

In general, painful though it was for those of us uncomfortable with cold-calling, the benefits of making all of those phone calls were well worth the effort. Where we did get a glimmer of encouragement to apply, it meant we had also made the tentative beginnings of building a relationship.

We had one spectacular success with this approach, with a Trust specializing in funding the education of science and engineering. When phoning I was fortunate enough to reach one of the founding Trustees who, initially sceptical of how supporting a Scout Group would meet their charitable aim, warmed to the idea when I explained just how much science and engineering we included in the termly programmes. As it happens, I and my cohorts have been often labelled as pyromaniacs, skip-raiders, mad-cap inventors and the like. All of which are probably true – nothing like demonstrating the art of chemical fire-lighting or skip-raiding lengths of four-by-two to build a giant marble-run. Or dismembering a dozen old petrol lawnmowers so the kids see how internal combustion engines work (tip – empty the carburettor of fuel beforehand to avoid unintentionally combining mechanical engineering with pyrotechnics).

So when I emailed the Trustee with all of the things we'd done which were vaguely related to science and engineering, the list was actually impressively long and varied. It ticked all of their right boxes too, for we received a very generous grant from them. We had built such a positive relationship from that initial phone call that when we held out our begging bowl for a second time, it was refilled with more than we'd asked for.

Pyromaniacs' Pleasure – an insight into the minds of our Leaders.

Do not try this at home, this is one for the campfire preferably when the kids have gone to bed.

Take a moderately large camp-fire and a tub of hot chocolate powder (or dried milk powder or equivalent, butterscotch flavour works well). Sprinkle powder above the flames. Your audience will gasp in wonder at the resulting fireball. In the interests of science, raid the kitchen tent for other foodstuffs to try. To make it really spectacular, borrow someone's tent pole and half-fill it with the powder. Position just above the flames and blow (not suck) hard. It is best that anyone on the opposite side of the fire has moved aside before you blow.

The unsolicited letter (or email) of introduction

Without doubt this was our least-successful way to reach donors. Sometimes, though, when the only information we had was either a postal or email address, it was the only option available to us. An email was generally the last resort. It's reasonable to suppose that these kinds of organizations get dozens – maybe hundreds – of approaches for funding and it is extremely difficult to make your email stand out from the crowd. A letter is better from that point of view – it can be personalized (a hand-written top and tail shows it's not entirely a mailshot) and we included some photos and supporting materials as well. We also kept the letter to one page and made it very clear in the opening paragraph why we were writing.

We tried different variants of this, from a scattergun mailshot to local businesses to including a reply-paid envelope. None of them really worked to generate additional funds and overall the cost of postage exceeded the amount we got back.

We got a much better rate of return when we wrote looking for specific materials. For example, we wrote to window companies to ask if they would discount the supply and installation of energy-efficient double-glazing. We wrote to insulation manufacturers asking about the supply of cavity and ceiling insulation. The success rate here was pretty much 100% - out of the half-dozen companies we approached for each component then one would always come up trumps. We always offered publicity in return (since this was pretty much all we could offer other than the dubious value of a bunch of Scouts to clean their cars) and consequently formed good working relationships with them. This had advantages when it came to actually constructing the building and the timetable became more aspirational than actual.

Our other hunting grounds

The whole "find the funder" task became an unending challenge – a combination of detective game and treasure-hunt. It actually, bizarrely, became quite fun, and very satisfying when funds flowed in from an unexpected direction. In no particular order we also looked at:

- Similar projects
- Local or known benefactors
- Local media
- Local government
- Supporting organizations
- Well-publicized sources
- On our doorstep

Similar projects

It is surprisingly easy to find out who has funded similar projects. I once spent a useful afternoon Googling "Scout Huts built in the last three years" and got more hits than I was expecting. Many of these had their own websites which often described the build process and occasionally listed how they had funded their project. When this wasn't included then a Group Scout Leader to Group Scout Leader email or phone call usually provided the information – most Groups are proud of their achievements and want to share their success. Our Group is no different – every organization contributing to our project is listed on our website. Described as a somewhat naïve thing to do ("why would you want to advertise that", we were once told at a funding conference), we reasoned that if this information can help other similar projects then why not. Besides which, we only listed the organization once we had received its funding, so no chance of compromising our own applications.

Local or known benefactors

There are a few funders who specialize in funding Scout and Guide Groups. This makes an approach to them a no-brainer with a high likelihood of success.

We also have in our area, a Foundation known for its generous support of Scouting. Founded by a (now) knight of the realm, it has donated large sums to Gilwell and also other Scouting causes. It's worth describing our approach since if ever there's an advertisement for good old-fashioned talking then this is it.

The Foundation has a website and on it is listed the current areas of interest of the Trustees. Reading these, it became obvious that our project fell well outside their criteria. On the face of it, we had no chance. However, we played the Scouting angle. Via a phone call to the Foundation's secretary, we were advised to write a letter to Sir P… explaining what we were doing, as he had discretionary power over how funding was allocated. The letter was written, enclosing some background information. Next thing, at 9pm one evening as I am reversing my car into a parking-space at a hotel, I get a phone call. Recognizing my local area code but not the number, I am greeted with "hello it's P... here". "P...?" I reply. "Yes", he says, " Sir P...". At which point I realized who it was and started babbling. "Ah yes, Sir P..., nice to hear from you how are you can I just finish parking my car so we can have a conversation nice to hear from you good of you to call nice to hear from you...".

Eventually we had an hour-long conversation in which I was able to explain what we were trying to do. It helped that there were common areas; he had been a keen Scout which he regarded as character-forming and life-changing so the conversation flowed easily. It concluded with him offering the amount we had asked for saying, "don't suppose the bloody Trustees will like it but it's my money and I'll tell them I want to do it!" Two phone calls and a letter had resulted in the second-largest donation our project received and a large bunch of flowers was sent to the secretary of the Foundation.

Local media

It paid, we found, to watch the local press to see who was building what. We discovered a firm demolishing a building had donated funding for furniture for a local playgroup. Well, we needed furniture as well – to the Google to find out the managing director and what their corporate social and community policy looked like. We were ultimately unsuccessful but it was worth the punt. We were more successful after we'd read that a community hall in a neighbouring village had been funded in part by an energy company. Although it required another rubber tape-measure to fall into their catchment area, they were very nice about it and donated substantial funds for our low-energy lighting.

Local Government

By which I mean County and Borough Councils. Both Reigate and Banstead Borough Council (RBBC) and Surrey County Council (SCC) had, at the time of application, grants available for capital building projects (in the case of SCC this was through its Leader's Initiative fund). These were refreshingly simple to both find information on, and subsequently to apply for. With both of these we built up a good relationship, which had two advantages:

- Although unsuccessful the first time of application we received valuable feedback that this wasn't due to the quality of our submission or because we didn't meet the funding criteria. We were unsuccessful because each felt that our project wasn't sufficiently advanced to be certain of using the funds in the current financial year – i.e. our application was premature. We were encouraged to submit another application closer to when we would actually need the funding.
- We received a "heads up" that there was funding available at the end of the year due, ironically, to other applicants failing to meet drawdown deadlines. It was suggested we apply for this; we duly did and received unexpected but most welcome bonus funding.

The quid pro quo was that we offered our new Scout Hall to showcase some activities during RBBC's week-long "Be Active" event for local young people. This we were more than happy to do – not only did this fit well into Scouting but also gave us the opportunity to show off our new hall.

Supporting organizations

In our treasure-hunt for funders we came across another group of organizations whose aim in life is to help and support voluntary groups, often to find funding for projects. In our case these included Reigate and Banstead Voluntary Service (RBVS)[2], Surrey Community Action (SCA), Community Foundation for Surrey (CFS), and Surrey Clubs for Young People (SCYP). All of these organizations provided useful sources of funding information and I guess that there are similar bodies across most of the UK. All without exception

---

[2] Now called Voluntary Action Reigate and Banstead

were skilled, enthusiastic, and highly supportive of what we were trying to achieve.

In the case of SCA, they try to match requirements to funders and then act on behalf of the funder to steer the application process and if successful, to process the post-project feedback.

RBVS usefully had access to commercial funding databases and ran searches on our behalf similar to the criteria we'd used with Funding Central. Although there was a considerable overlap in output, there were additional organizations identified to whom we were eligible to apply.

Most of these organizations went beyond just providing sources of funding. For example, CFS has helped us with practicalities around risk assessments, and some of the minutiae around operating a community building. Although we have yet to take advantage, SCYP can supply equipment for activities and there is the possibility of reciprocal visits to different youth groups. Consistent with our belief in the power of talk, we spent a long time discussing our requirements with these organizations either face-to-face or on the phone in order to start to build awareness and the relationship.

Well-publicized sources

Comic Relief, The National Lottery, and The People's Postcode are all well-known sources of funding and attract national publicity. It's very easy to be lulled into thinking that an application is bound to be successful to these kinds of bodies because they have loads of money and it ticks most of their boxes. We found the reality is rather different: each receives so many applications the process is (maybe deliberately?) extremely lengthy, time-consuming, and quite frankly off-putting to go through.

One of our Leaders, in a former life, wrote some of the evaluation criteria for National Lottery funding applications. Faced with their 20-page application form and his advice, we decided not to bother applying: we would have struggled to provide evidence of community need, at the time one of the major decision factors behind an award of funding, and we felt our time and energy would be better spent on applications with a greater chance of success.

Having said that, ironically one of the simplest applications we made was to Awards for All – Lottery funding for smaller projects. This not only had a refreshingly simple application process but from submission to notification of success to money actually in the bank took around four weeks, which was pretty much a record. Our case might have been helped by being specific for what the funding was to be used for, i.e. it wasn't just disappearing into the general building fund but there would be something tangible to look at.

On our doorstep

Sometimes sources of funding were closer than we realized. Towards the start of our research we had sent a plea to our parents to let us know if their place of work offered any matched funding for community projects or any other form of support. This was remarkably successful and led to our first four-figure grant and some other funding, some free temporary storage, some free labour to help with the fit-out (in exchange for beer and a barbeque) and, via a scheme to allow its employees to take on a voluntary project for up to two days and be paid for it, all of the tiling in the washrooms.

Step 2)   Ask them nicely for money

With our initial list of targets written down our focus changed to how we would best turn an approach into cash (or cash equivalent). There were some obvious hurdles:

- We had little experience of doing this (when we started, we hadn't come across the Supporting Organizations mentioned above)
- We had no track record of success (with the exception of a modest investment of Group reserves to kick-start the feasibility study, the building fund started pretty much from zero)

- We had no prior relationship with any of the organizations we would be approaching

Supporting information

I mentioned on page 7 that when we approached the Diocese to ask for a lease, we had adopted a business-like and professional approach, focusing on the benefits and leaving out the emotion of the cause. It seemed to us that anyone considering an investment (for that's what it is) in our project would want to know the basics – the why, what, when, how - covering the benefits, costs, organization, qualifications, experience and so on. They would, we reasoned, want to be reassured that their money was going to the right place and would be used properly. By viewing the approach as presenting an investment opportunity, it became obvious to us that what we needed was very similar to a business plan. This was something we did have experience of writing.

Our starting point was to prepare a document covering the basics: a summary of the proposal, why the project was needed, the project finances, benefits, expected outcomes and so on. The box Our Project Proposal Contents on the following page shows the contents of the document we wrote, which ended up being about 25 pages long and included, on the front cover, a photograph of the garages we would demolish and an artist's impression of what the finished product would look like. When neatly spiral-bound the document looked attractive and professional, and we also published it electronically so that it could be emailed if necessary.

We were careful to assure the accuracy and veracity of the information we included, and ensured that if challenged we would be able to refer back to the source information. For example, when describing our demography, the information was taken from our latest Scout Association census return, and that the range of activities we said we delivered to young people was taken from a review of termly programmes from the previous few years. We were also careful not to overstate the benefits or to set unfeasible success factors.

We had taken the conscious decision to include a lot of information in it as we felt (again in our naivety) that for each funding application we could just tweak it a bit but the bulk of the document would remain the same. We soon learned that this was wrong – that criteria for funders are specific to their aims and not generic; therefore, there was no such thing as one size to fit all. So although we had a base document we ended up tailoring it in pretty much every case to change the emphasis. For example, when we were applying more for community funding as opposed to funding for a Scout Group then we would emphasise the benefits to the local

---

Our Project Proposal Contents

1 SUMMARY
2 BACKGROUND
2.1 A brief history
2.2 Our accommodation problem
2.3 Endorsement of proposal
2.4 Our demography and inclusivity
2.5 Opportunities for young people
2.6 Our role in the local community
3 PROPOSAL
3.1 What we are seeking to build.
3.2 Where this will be built
3.3 Timetable and organization
3.4 Communications
3.5 Project costs and fund-raising
3.6 Measuring success
4 BENEFITS
4.1 Benefits to our young people
4.2 Benefits to our Scout Group
4.3 Benefits to the community
5 PROJECT CONTACTS
APPENDIX 1: SITE LOCATION
APPENDIX 2: OUTLINE BUILDING PLAN
APPENDIX 3: RANGE OF ACTIVITIES

---

community, its development opportunities, social cohesion, the breadth of community users the project would benefit and so on. If we were applying to a funder whose aims lay in supporting youth groups then we would stress the benefits of Scouting on a young person's development, the increased adventurous opportunities the project would generate, and the increased opportunities for adult volunteering.

The document thus evolved as our experience with funding applications developed. There were two other changes:

- We produced a summary proposal – a four-page document covering the main topics – and a one-page summary. These were in part driven by funders' guidelines stipulating the maximum length of supporting documents and (for the one-pager) a document we could easily and cheaply include with a letter of introduction.

- We removed the project costs and fund-raising section and included them separately. Anathema that a business plan should make no reference to costs but done purely for practicality: we were sending out this proposal during a time in which our project costs were still being refined and we had started to have some success with funding applications. Thus these data were changing. Constantly revising costs in the main document to reflect the amount raised and the amount still required became, quite frankly, a pain in the neck so costs were removed to a separate document linked to our cost and funding tracker spreadsheets and updated automatically. Plus, some funding applications required a separate submission of project budget so in effect we killed two birds with one stone and made administration simpler.

Making the application

I attended a funding conference in which one of the speakers was from a well-established funding organization and gave an insight into the process behind evaluating grant applications. Two things stuck in my mind:

- The volume of applications received by some organizations is so great that each gets around thirty seconds for its initial evaluation. If it doesn't stand out, then it gets rejected.

- That nothing is more irritating to a funder than when, having published guidelines on how to structure an application and what to include, these are ignored by the applicant. The presenter was very clear in her advice: if the guidelines say apply by letter with maximum length of two pages then that's what needs to be sent in (and no cheap tricks such as using 6pt font to get more words on the page.). If they ask for supporting financial information, then include it. Ignore this advice at your peril, she said, send in three pages when two is the maximum or forget to include the project budget when requested then you can expect only one result: rejection.

As harsh as these both sound, they are not unreasonable. Any funder will tell you that they get so many applications that no matter how worthy or laudable the cause, they cannot support every one and they receive more than enough which do comply with their funding guidelines not to waste time on those which don't.

Before we committed pen to paper or finger to keyboard, we usually double-checked the funding guidelines to make sure we knew what information to include. Not all applications were started from scratch – often there would be similarities in the information sought (for example, almost all asked "please describe your project") so we could re-use parts of previous applications. Step 5 explains how we organized our applications though this didn't entirely obviate frustration at knowing the exact words needed had been written before but being unable to find them.

On occasion we needed to do additional research before submitting an application. This was particularly true with our local government applications which usually required explaining how our project met its community objectives or complemented its vision for increasing social diversity or whatever. This meant we had to understand the current policies and priorities, which in turn meant we had to find out about them. Most of this information was readily available on their websites or from our local library and provided many of the answers needed (as well as a cure for insomnia).

I stated earlier that there are many books on writing funding applications, which deal with what to say and how to say it, the tone, the style, ensuring that the application reads well, is spell-checked and grammatically correct and so on. These are well-worth reading and another pearl of advice from within one of them was that if you are unfamiliar with making these kinds of applications then give them to someone to proof-read before they are submitted.

> **A helpful gem**
>
> All of the books we used are referenced in the bibliography but there was a gem among them, nothing to do with the art of fund-raising. *"Type and Layout: How Topography and Design Can Get Your Message Across - Or get in the Way"* explains how font, line-spacing, the use of colour and so on has a profound impact on the readability of a document and a reader's ability to assimilate its information. Reading this resulted in revisions in the presentation of some of our marketing information.

Although we seldom received direct feedback on the quality of our applications we were successful around 12% of the time – above the industry average apparently – so we must have been doing something right. I attribute our success to:

- Having experience of writing business plans, so we knew the style and content to use.
- Being very clear about the benefits and how the application would meet the funders' aims
- Being specific on how the funding would be used
- Being passionate but not emotional. No-one is a better advocate for your project than yourself.

We continued this approach across all of the applications we made, whether by online application form or letter, whether for actual funding or goods/services in kind, when speaking directly to a funder or communicating by email. We achieved, I think, a high degree of consistency in our approach which further vindicated, if such was necessary, making this part of our fund-raising the responsibility of a small number of people and giving them autonomy and authority to apply for funding without recourse to Executive Committee agreement.

Step 3) Expect the cheque, naturally by return mail

Okay so now we were being really naïve. Having sent off a flood of applications, we metaphorically sat back and waited for the cheques to drop through the letterbox. Which of course they didn't, at least for a long time and thus our eyes were opened to other facets of the grant application process:

- We never heard back from at least half of the applications we'd made. No acknowledgement of receipt, no rejection, no "it's being considered and we'll revert in due course". Nothing, nada, zippo. This was immensely frustrating. I know it's a buyer's market and these organizations get a lot of applications but the administration overhead of a sending a boilerplate acknowledgement or rejection wouldn't kill them, especially if sent at zero cost by email.

- There is a long gestation period. Many application guidelines give the timetable for either submissions or when Trustees will review and decide. When these are not given it becomes a lottery on when an application will be reviewed. There is no legal requirement around the frequency when Trustees should meet, and many review funding applications just once per year, especially the smaller charities. Usually there is no way of knowing when their Trustee meeting will be held which means across all applications you could be waiting an average of six months and possibly over a year before hearing, assuming that you hear anything at all. This isn't universal – many do meet more regularly but that's usually because they have so many applications to review.

- No-one likes to be first. Many guidelines advise not to apply until a minimum level of funding has been achieved, sometimes an amount, sometimes a percentage of the total project cost. Which of course rather becomes a vicious circle – you cannot get funding because you haven't got funds already, and because you haven't raised funds already then your application for funding won't be successful. In our case we were helped by some modest pump-priming from existing Group reserves and also that our own internal fund-raising was hitting its stride early on, both of which did start to accumulate money in the bank. Nonetheless, it took us one year to raise the first third of our target but the remaining two-thirds all came in the second year.

Occasionally when we hadn't heard then we would phone the contact name, assuming we had that information, and ask them politely for confirmation of receipt. Which led to another eye-opener: the administration of many charities is handled by legal advisers, for example solicitors or Trustee departments in banks. Other than confirming that application has been passed onto the Trustees, often they could offer little other information other than "you'll hear if you're successful". Eventually we gave up doing this as it was adding no value – we simply had to learn the art of patience.

Sometimes, as well, news of success came from a strange direction. I have previously described how we applied to Surrey County Council (SCC) under its Leader's Initiative fund. We knew from the application process when the applications were being reviewed. Being a local government body, SCC very efficiently publishes the Minutes of its committee meetings on its website albeit buried pretty deep. But Tony, who is adept at ferreting out information, managed to locate the respective Minutes and found out that we had been recommended for award of the grant. Great news, we thought, but hold on... recommendation isn't the same thing as approval. This was to be given (or not) at another meeting chaired by the Leader of SCC – a County Councillor. What we also noticed was that this next meeting was open to the public, so one wintery afternoon John and I turned up suited and booted at County Hall to hear our fate. We were ushered into the committee room and when we asked where we should sit, we were told that it didn't really matter since we were the first members of the public to ever have attended the meeting! But being there in person helped. Ours was the first application to be considered, we were able to answer some questions from the Chairman who within minutes had given his approval for funding and said very complimentary things about what we were doing and that he'd appreciated that we'd bothered to go along. For our project this grant was a milestone as it took us beyond the 90% we needed for construction to start.

Step 4) Write them a letter of thanks

Of course, when a cheque does arrive, or the letter confirming a successful application, or (occasionally) a phone call saying "just wanted to let you know…", this is a time of great and smug satisfaction. When the first cheque dropped through my letterbox we were euphoric – this was dancing in the street time. That it was for a fairly modest amount made no difference. It meant we had been successful – we had convinced an organization we'd previously never heard of to support us. It meant that what we had written in our proposal made sense; it ticked the right boxes and had made a compelling case. It meant, most significantly, that our approach worked. Until this moment, given Step 3)'s uncertainty over response and response-time, we did not know if what we were doing was right. When the first cheque arrived, we knew for sure and could be pretty certain that other success would follow. This we shouted to the world from the rooftops.

It goes almost without saying that any award should be promptly acknowledged. We also introduced a personal touch. One of our Scouts was gifted at drawing Manga characters, so I asked him to produce a card which showed a Beaver, Cub, Scout, and Explorers with a simple "thank you" and a brief message inside saying how the donor's support had made a difference. When replying to solicitors or third-party Trust administrators we would always ask that our thank-you card was passed to the Trustees.

I have mentioned previously that all successful donors were added to a page on our website; we have gone further than this in our new hall and created a board of fame – a wallboard constructed of salvaged mahogany which contains name-plaques listing all of our supporters and donors. Although we don't expect that we will ever meet many of our funders personally,

Picture by Dominic Doran, aged 13 (then)

we think it important that any visitors to the hall will see the level of support we attained.

Step 5) Try and avoid asking them again

It becomes embarrassing and appears a tad careless when one re-applies to an organization which has already said no for valid reasons. Also a waste of our and their time and, depending on the reason for rejection, probably detrimental to any chance of re-application.

The way we managed the application process, who we'd applied to and the result, was fairly simple: on our Group shared drive we created a spreadsheet which recorded the organization and its contact details, the amount we'd applied for, the status of the application (see box Classification we used for managing applications) and a note of communications we'd had –

Classification we used for managing applications
1. To be checked
2. Awaiting response
3A. Eligible for application - now
3B. Eligible for application - future
4. Application made
5. Application funded
6A. Application unsuccessful
6B. Application assumed unsuccessful
7. No application - don't meet criteria

emails, phone calls, letters etc. There was also a "key dates" field into which was entered the date of, say, when the Trustees meet, which would give an indication of when we would be likely to hear. Using a spreadsheet meant we could also do fancy stuff such as generating a pivot table of application status – this meant we could have a stab at predicting the likelihood of future success and gear the application run-rate and the building construction timetable to that.

Another advantage from having all information recorded in one place was that it was easy to generate and refresh mailing lists when communicating progress. This is discussed more fully in Step 6 but communication would have been much more difficult and inconsistent had we needed to dig out contact details each time.

We also set up a simple folder structure on the shared drive which contained a copy of anything we'd sent to an organization. Where our proposal had been customized for a specific application, we would file a copy in that organization's folder along with scanned copies of correspondence. Not rocket science but basic organization which was difficult to get wrong. With hindsight we should have also filed a copy of emails sent to and received from an organization – trying to remember when an email had been sent and to whom became problematic. Fortunately, the search capabilities of Microsoft Outlook are pretty good and more reliable than mere memory.

Step 6) Communicate progress

We didn't restrict status updates to those who had supported us financially. We also included stakeholders, suppliers (both actual and prospective), support organizations, friends, family, and anyone even vaguely related to the project. Around once a quarter we would send out a newsletter which reminded everyone what the project was about, some headlines of accomplishments since the previous updates, and the planned activities in the next period. We also included a complete list of all of our donors and sponsors.

The reasons for distributing this far and wide were fourfold

- We felt we had an obligation to keep our sponsors and donors informed of how their money was being spent. Often this was a mandatory requirement of receiving their funding.
- We wanted to keep as big an audience as possible informed, so that they knew the project was for real and progressing towards a conclusion.
- We wanted anyone who had supported us, financially, practically, morally, or however to know their support counted, was appreciated, and moved us forward.
- There was a chance that our update would be forwarded on, raising the potential of further funding, or spark ideas of where additional funding might be sourced.

Our newsletter was produced as a one-page pdf document and sent by email. These were conscious choices – pdf is a universal format and a one-page document is easy to read and of modest size thus wouldn't clog up inboxes. Sending via email meant it was easy to forward on (the accompanying text always asked for the update to be sent to others involved in the organization's decision to support us) and easy to reply to when necessary.

In conclusion, what did we learn?

The process is time-consuming

Researching, contacting (often requiring repeated attempts), and completing applications is not a 5-minute task. On average it took half a day to complete an application, and some with the more complex application forms took much longer.

Patience, patience, patience

Having submitted an application, sit back and wait (and do some more applications). You may get an acknowledgement, but most of the time you won't. You may, like me, think this is wrong but that is just how it is. And you could be waiting up to a year.

How to stand out from the crowd

Your application needs to grab the attention of the assessor and stand out from the dozens (hundreds) they also receive. Doesn't mean the use of garish colours and amusing clipart, but does mean a clear and readable application which ticks the right boxes and is easy to assimilate.

Be alert throughout

Your research cannot stop, at least if you have an ongoing need to raise funds. Be on the constant lookout in all directions for similar projects and don't be shy to ask how they got their money.

Look close to home

Some funding will be available on your doorstep, whether through your own contacts, local government, local businesses and so on

Increase the chance of success

If appropriate, consider your charitable status and consider whether to register as a charity. As a UK Scout Group 17th Reigate has "excepted" charitable status which was sufficient for most, but not all, funding applications which asked for a charity number. Some would only consider registered charities and thus we were precluded from applying to these. With hindsight we should have registered as a charity in our own right, as a lot of Scout Groups do anyway, though this would not have been a decision to take lightly and without consultation.

It's good to talk

We spent a lot of time talking to prospective funders or people who could help us find them. All of this time we were building our relationship with them which paid dividends and would have been

	impossible if we'd stuck to emails or letters.
Give them (the funders) what they have asked for	*If you ignore the application guidelines or don't provide the information required in the format requested, then expect to be disappointed. Funders simply do not have the time (or probably inclination) to correct your mistakes – the onus is on you to get it right.*
Celebrate success	*When the cheque drops through the post-box or funds are transferred into your bank account or you get a letter pledging support then shout about it from the rooftops. Success breeds success – if one organization has supported you then others will follow*
Phone a friend	*We wish we'd uncovered much earlier the helpful organizations which exist to support voluntary bodies in their fund-raising. They are out there, staffed with knowledgeable and helpful people, so it makes sense to look for them and use them.*
Pick your targets carefully	*As per the first lesson learned above, applying for grants is very time-consuming. It thus pays to pick the*

targets carefully and where there is maximum chance of success. National charities are generous in their support for good causes but they will receive correspondingly more applications because they are well-known, and their selection criteria will be tougher.

Don't always ask for cash

For a building project such as ours, we knew as well as hard cash there would be plenty of other things we needed – materials, furniture, equipment, and so on. Sometimes it is easier for an organization to donate or discount these than give hard cash, especially if you are asking for products which they manufacture or distribute.

Be efficient at organization and administration

From day one have a system – manual, paper, electronic it matters not – in which you can keep track of your applications. This is exponentially more important the more applications you submit – it helps avoid mistakes and becomes invaluable when communicating progress.

Don't build first and ask for money afterwards

Most funding bodies will not fund work already completed. Which means being canny about the timing of some of the works and what the funding will be used for – there's no point in applying for funding towards the foundations if the concrete has already been poured. We were very careful to ensure that at the time a funding application was made, the potentially-funded work had not begun and we could demonstrate this on our building schedule.

Be like Oliver Twist

Success once does not preclude success again from the same source. There is nothing wrong in holding out the begging bowl for a second time, and in some ways it is easier since there is a relationship and support already established.

5 – GETTING IT BUILT

This isn't a chapter on construction techniques or how to plan and execute a building project. Nor is it an exercise on quantity-surveying or detailed cost planning or any of the other myriad skills needed for successful construction. Instead, it describes the approach we took, once most of the money was in place, to actually getting our hall built and opened and deals with some of the hurdles we had to overcome on the way.

The legal niceties

I have described in Chapter 1 – Getting Started how we had successfully negotiated a fifty-year lease on the land on which we wanted to build with the landlords, the Diocese of Arundel and Brighton. As it turned out, this was only the start of the process. Firstly, this intent had to be translated into an agreed Heads of Terms which had to be accepted by the Charities Commission (all to do with disposal of an asset – the land – by one charity – the Diocese – to another charity – us). Then we had to agree the terms of the Agreement for Lease itself, and this is where the pain started.

We announced to the world in January 2014 that we had raised enough money for construction to start, and that we were planning to start building two months later. We had assumed this would be long enough to dot i's and cross t's on the lease. Were we naïve or what. Mainly for two reasons:

- We had underestimated the glacial pace of the legal profession
- It turned out that some of the original stakeholders who had given their support hadn't thought that we were serious about the project. Thus when we announced the funding was in place to start, some of them woke up and got all agitated and worried about what we were doing.

It took a further seven months, hours and hours of extracurricular meetings, and tens of thousands of pounds of unbudgeted legal and professional fees to Diocesan advisers to get to the point where we could start building. During this time, we had to:

- Refine the design multiple times concerning the layout of storage to be leased back to the Parish
- Refine the costs multiple times to ensure all of the major cost items were covered and justify why normally-expected costs had been omitted (for example there was no crane hire cost included because we had an alternate way of lifting roof trusses into position)
- Provide evidence of contingency funding should our costs over-run (both Parish and Diocese were concerned not to be left with a half-finished building)
- Revise the layout of the car-park multiple times to demonstrate that there would be a net loss of only two parking spaces
- Chalk the outline of the new building and car-parking onto the plot to prove that it fitted within the site boundaries
- Accept a management agreement which defined how the Scout Hall would operate in conjunction with the new Parish Centre (containing, for example, an anti-poaching clause to prevent us from taking rental business away from the Parish Centre)
- And much more…

We also had to defend our budget against a professional opinion that the building would cost at least three times what we had estimated, based on current per-square-metre commercial construction rates. In my speech at the opening ceremony I couldn't let this pass, making reference to this professional cost estimation and that we had indeed completed our build for 40% of it. One of the few occasions when the phrase "yah boo we were right" has been heard in a speech!

One might read this list and think that none of what was being requested of us was overly unreasonable. This was in fact our view too; what we found frustrating almost to the point of giving up was the timing of having to provide all of this information. This could have easily been done with much less stress in parallel with the two years it had taken us to raise the money. It was undoubtedly the lowest point in the project and took a lot of the shine away from having raised an extraordinary amount of money in a short space of time.

But then suddenly we had the magic signatures on the lease documents; our anguish and frustration was forgotten and the demolition team moved in to start. My happy-grumpy chart (see reference to this on page 32 in respect to our super-six Explorer hikers) had swung upwards again towards the smiley face.

The design process

Well, we knew sort of what we wanted right from the start: basically a simple rectangular box with an entrance lobby and washrooms at one end, a kitchen, and plenty of storage. And a meeting hall with as much floor-space as we could squeeze into the land available. We wanted no fancy architectural features or curves, no expensive finishes, no fragile fixings. We wanted a utilitarian building suitable for a multitude of uses both Scouting and community. It had to be secure, for the safety of the young people using it. It had to be energy-efficient beyond the minimum requirements, to reduce its running costs. It had to comply, obviously, with the latest building regulations including disabled access. We had to be mindful of the requirement of the lease to return to the Parish the equivalent storage and garaging which we were demolishing. Above all we wanted simplicity.

Which leads nicely onto one of the early decisions we needed to make. The original intention was simply to add a first floor above the existing garages and storage, and to kind of tack on entrance facilities at one end. Our Explorers, aided by a mini-digger, spent a long time digging trial holes to assess the depth and width of the existing foundations and the conclusion by our structural engineer was that they were insufficient without underpinning. So we reverted to plan B, which was to demolish to slab level and build new. Although more expensive, this had some advantages:

- We could vary the footprint to better suit our requirements
- Being a new build would qualify materials to be zero-rated for VAT[3], saving us money
- We would get a building whose structural integrity was uncompromised from ground-up

The design process evolved as the project progressed, although comparing the original set of plans with what we actually built shows not much difference which means we got it pretty much correct initially. One significant change we did make inside was to sacrifice some of the storage to create another meeting room on the ground floor. This was a good call – we managed to create a 30m² room which has proven invaluable, giving us the flexibility to run simultaneous meetings as well as another facility which can be used by community groups.

The plans were drafted by a designer mate of David's who did a fantastic job. That he was based in Paris and thus all communication was via email proved no barrier. Changes were made quickly and accurately and his detailed knowledge of UK building regulations ensured compliance as demanded. But to this day he has not actually seen in person what he designed!

Another mate of David's, a professional structural engineer, did all of the steelwork design pro bono, a decision he might have later rued as to stiffen the building to within acceptable tolerances meant the design was very complex and required a small battleship's worth of steel.

Some of the other design features and considerations are described over the next few pages.

---

[3] Under HMRC rules at the time

Nipping off the corner

When excavating the footings for the new foundations Michael, our contract digger driver, hit something solid in one of the rear corners. Thankfully his 3-tonne digger had not broken it for when the clay was scraped away we discovered a large pipe bisecting where the corner of the foundations would be. It was at least 300mm in diameter, made of solid black plastic, and had an enormous coupling where two lengths obviously joined together. This pipe was not on any of the site plans, nor did it appear on the title deeds as an easement. We were somewhat baffled, until a piece of tape was spotted in the ground nearby suggesting it was a sewer-pipe. It was more difficult than might be imagined to establish ownership but further investigation via the local water company eventually confirmed that it was actually a high-pressure water pipe. Just as well then that the digger had not gone through it else we could have been responsible for closing the London to Brighton train line, a mere 10m away from the pipe.

The problem we then had was what to do about it, since clearly it couldn't be moved without a tremendous amount of work and cost. Nor could we build over it – the water company's regulations prevented that. So we ended up taking off the corner of the building such that the brickwork runs parallel to the pipe, allowing access to the pipe if needed. It's given a rather odd shape to the back corner of the building and subsequently made fitting the internal staircase somewhat tricky, but definitely the lesser of two evils.

There was a postscript in that when the water company looked again they decided that it wasn't a water pipe but rather a high-pressure sewer pipe as the label had originally indicated. This meant a different set of regulations applied and would have required us to construct much further away from it. This would have massively compromised the building footprint and in reality jeopardised the feasibility of the entire design. However, as we had their original ruling (that it was a water pipe) in an email and the foundations had by then been poured, they relented and confirmed we could carry on. We had dodged another bullet and demonstrated the wisdom of getting important decisions in writing.

Toilets

I have often commented that the role of Scout Leader often involves many skills which never appear in the role description, and becoming experts in the design and regulations of toilets in a community building definitely wasn't in there. Tony's job takes him to customers all over the UK, mine takes me to offices around Europe. When we compared notes we found we were both doing the same thing on our travels: taking an unhealthy interest in the design of washroom facilities in all of the locations we visited. Ratio of urinals to estimated number of workers, whether the facilities were unisex, the square meterage per cubicle, full-length or part-length cubicle doors, provision for disabled users, position of the hot-air hand-drier in respect to the washbasin, soap dispenser or bottle of squirty soap, provision for cleaning materials and so on. Most importantly for those longer visits, was the motion-sensor (no pun intended) on the lights set for sufficient duration to prevent "customers" being plunged into darkness at an inopportune moment[4]. On more than one occasion I was interrupted whilst counting floor-tiles to get an idea of room dimensions. To my professional colleagues this must have looked a little weird and quite frankly disturbing, and wasn't easy to explain to the French or Germans exactly why I was doing this.

This was all necessary since the professionals advising the Parish on the content of the lease weren't happy with our proposal for unisex loos. We studied BS6465[5] avidly to understand the regulations and what we wanted to do was perfectly permissible, however as we were at the time fighting battles on multiple

---

[4] In order, the conclusions were roughly: 1 per 25 (male) workers, only in Scandinavia, about 2m², mostly full-length, normal expected provision, as close as permitted, and soap dispensers attached to the wall. And for those longer visits, a timer on the lights set for a delay between 3 minutes (risky) and 20 minutes (safe but might render facility temporarily uninhabitable).

[5] BS 6465-1:2006. Sanitary installations – Part 1: Code of practice for the design of sanitary facilities and scales of provision of sanitary and associated appliances

fronts we compromised with separate cubicles for males and females and a separate unisex disabled loo. No complaints from users thus far.

Waste tank

Flushed with the finalization of the toilet design, we had to work out what to do with the end product, as it were. We had a problem with levels on the site in that the nearest foul drain was above our ground-level. We had another foul drain available at the bottom of a steep slope to the side of the building. This was our preferred option until ruled out by the water company on the basis that the gradient was too steep and waste products would pick up too much velocity. Now there's an image to conjure with.

We were thus left with the option of tapping into the foul drain above the level of the site, which required some form of pumped storage system (a simple cess-pit was ruled out as we couldn't site it sufficiently far from the building). Cue David becoming an expert on the different types of systems available, their capacities, flow-rates, capacity of pumps for handling "solids", pipe connections and so on. Another case of learning things you'd never thought you needed to know. In the end the solution was quite straightforward – a tank buried in the ground with a pipe in from the building waste and two pumps (one for backup) discharging the contents via a 100mm pipe buried under the car-park into the main foul drain.

We did the installation ourselves, initially burying the tank 300mm too shallow so the top wasn't covered and the tank inlet was above the building outlet. It was a massive effort to dig it back out as the clay had settled and we could not break the suction. We did try using ropes and our Group minibus to haul it out but all this achieved was a strong smell of burning clutch (we later sold the minibus). We got there in the end using spades, dug the hole a bit deeper, and settled it at the correct depth. Then we had to commission the system and test it and somewhere there is a photo of three of us looking on as the tank discharged its contents into the foul drain for the first time. Seldom have even new parents been prouder.

Security

Security for young people using the building was my top design consideration. With the main hall being on the first floor and the loos on the ground floor next to the entrance lobby, we had to ensure that a) no-one who shouldn't be in the building could get into the building, and b) it would be difficult for young people to wander outside unbeknown to the leaders. Whatever system was implemented should also be able to control access to various parts of the building whilst at the same time being simple to use. A complicated or inconvenient system would tend to be bypassed, thus negating the whole idea behind it.

We were fortunate to work with a local security company who provided us with exactly what we needed. Entry through most doors is controlled by magnetic locks which require a fob to enter and a button to leave. It is connected to the building alarm system making it simple to control. There are video intercoms on the building entrance doors which signal into the main hall when someone wants to come into the building, and the corresponding magnetic locks can be released from upstairs. This means when parents collect after the end of a meeting, leaders can control access to the building without leaving the main hall.

Some parents have made "Fort Knox" style comments, especially if they are left outside in the rain (the idea for a rain-porch was abandoned due to cost – the message was if it's raining then bring an umbrella). Our counter to those comments is to ask whether they would prefer no security and the option for anyone to wander unchallenged into the building containing their children.

Audio-visual facilities

We wanted a building able to cope with not only the traditional activities of Scouting but also those in the 21ˢᵗ century. More and more activities now have a portion of their content on-line, and a lot of training is similarly delivered via the Internet.

We also knew that from Beavers to Explorers they like to perform, whether as part of an AGM entertainment, or a talent show, or describing their hobbies to the rest of the Group, or providing feedback on an Expedition Hike or whatever. We were determined that facilities to enable all of this should be there from day one.

We created a permanent "stage" area at one end of the hall simply by finishing our salvaged oak flooring three metres from the end and continuing with a carpeted area. Happily, this coincided exactly with the amount of oak flooring we had available. This different finish effectively demarcates the "stage", above which we have hung lighting bars with a variety of coloured flood and spotlights. One of our former Scouts (who also happens to be one of my sons) now designs theatre sound and light systems, so he put together and commissioned an extremely good audio-visual system capable of taking a wide variety of media inputs and outputting via a high-definition projector and speakers above the "stage". This has proved immensely popular during sleepovers when our Beavers have been allowed to stay up until midnight watching cartoons from their sleeping-bags.

Unbeknown to John, our audio-visual setup also included a TV tuner in order to show programmes on the big screen. He only became aware of this when he spotted the satellite dish on the wall behind the building. Why, he wanted to know, did we have the ability to show TV programmes? Who in their right mind, he continued to rant, would want to come to watch TV in a Scout Hall? Well, I argued, there are lots of programmes – survival series, wildlife documentaries, nature and geography programmes – which might be of interest to some of our young people and useful within Scouting activities. It was of course entirely coincidental that the first time we used this facility with an audience was to watch the 2016 Rugby World Cup Final.

Staircase and balustrade

Although we wanted a utilitarian building, we indulged ourselves with the staircase and installed one custom-made from light oak. This wasn't purely for vanity; the staircase is the first thing seen when anyone enters the building and we wanted not only a 'wow' factor, but also a staircase that will last the lifetime of the building and need re-varnishing maybe only every five years. A softwood staircase would have been substantially cheaper but wouldn't have stood up as well to the constant battering from children's feet and would have needed re-painting and maintaining every year to avoid looking scruffy.

We made the balustrades ourselves. Behind the altar at St. Joseph's church is a stained-glass window based on the tree of life. It has wonderfully intricate lead-work so, taking a photo of it, we managed to reproduce it in metalwork for the balustrades. Over the summer months this involved another of my sons learning a) how to weld and b) how to bend steel bar into intricate curves but the effort was worthwhile – it looks fantastic, is unique, and is an association with our church.

Kitchen

Kitchens are kitchens are kitchens. We wanted a practical kitchen that had space and facilities for both teaching cooking skills to the young people and could cope with preparing food for social or fund-raising events. We were fortunate that a local company donated all of the cupboards and work-surfaces, and one of our grant applications met the cost of all of the appliances. In the end the only things we had to buy ourselves were the tiles for the walls and the stainless-steel hand-washing sink. The most popular appliance? The hot-water boiler ensuring a constant supply of boiling water for tea.

One of the best things we designed in from the start was a large serving hatch between kitchen and main hall. Protected by an electric roller-shutter it is invaluable for serving drinks to the kids mid-way through a meeting.

The fire escape

I mentioned on page 48 that we had done Section-specific fund-raising to raise money for the fire-escape. With the main hall on the first floor, a safe way of exiting the building in an emergency was a mandatory requirement.

We could have had a steel escape custom-fabricated, however we're a Scout Group and that's not our way. Some quick research from David on a popular online auction site showed steel fire-escapes were often sold as salvaged from buildings being demolished. After a bit of patience, a suitable one came up and we won the bid. A kind haulier collected it for us and stored it in his yard for several months then delivered it to site when we were ready to install it. This was the first time we'd actually seen what we'd bought and the best way of describing it is to imagine a two-tonne Meccano kit. It was massive – large sections of galvanized steel which individually weighed loads and required an army of blokes to move around. It was also fabricated 180 degrees the wrong way round, 2m too long for our requirements, and missing an upright support. This wasn't a massive problem as everything bolted together and mostly we could unbolt panels and re-fix them to the other side. The excess length was solved with an angle grinder and we had the missing support fabricated.

The real challenge was lifting it into position. Even with unbolting most of the treads the frame weighed close to a tonne and we had to lift it and bolt it to the wall 2.5m above the ground. Of course, the easiest way would have been to pay our nice haulier to come back and hold it into position using his Hiab lifter, again however we're a Scout Group and that's not our way. We do pioneering projects, we thought. We build rope bridges and A-frames and swings and all sorts of stuff. This is a similar challenge, we convinced ourselves, only a bit bigger.

Our first idea was to use the winch on a jeep, with the cable taken up and over a roof-beam in the hall and attached to the fire-escape frame. When the winch started it certainly moved the frame but due to the angles involved, the frame became a giant wrecking-ball heading at speed towards the building. We quickly stopped to re-think.

The second, third, and fourth attempts all involved trying to jack up or lever the frame in position. None were successful and much time was spent with blokes standing around it looking thoughtful, drinking tea, and scratching parts of their anatomy.

We nailed it on the fifth attempt. Earlier we had bought (David, popular online auction site) some steel scaffold towers so we could reach to paint the ceiling in the main hall. We erected one of these to the side of the frame, ran a piece of left-over structural steel as a beam across the top to inside the fire-escape doorway, and cranked the frame into position using a chain winch. Bit hairy to operate the chain winch as it meant standing almost under the frame whilst it was being raised, but we managed it without incident and bolted the frame to the wall. We were fortunate to find Ian, a superb welder and ace bloke, who helped fit the rest of the panels and handrails and now it's impossible to recognize it as the same thing which arrived as a jumble of parts on the back of a lorry. Total cost under a grand – a quarter of the price of a custom fabrication and as a bonus we got a ready-made mounting for a basketball hoop.

Managing the budget

I described earlier on page 13 how we constructed the budget for the construction, omitting only the value of the volunteer labour which we knew would be available and wasn't costing hard money. In essence we budgeted in two halves. Firstly, to get us to the point of a watertight shell – the basic building structure completed, the roof on, the doors and windows installed. Secondly, to do the internal fit-out – first- and second-fix electrical and mechanical, stud walls, internal finishes, flooring and so on.

We were pretty spot on with our budgeting to complete the water-tight shell. Much of this work was fixed-price from sub-contractors or was based on firm quotes. We only came unstuck in a few places. The zinc roof was more expensive as the price of raw materials had increased between original quote and actual installation (nearly a year between the two), and we needed more concrete than originally estimated. The shape and levels of the site made it difficult to estimate the concrete volume accurately and despite most of it being donated, we had to purchase additional. We also needed much more structural steel than originally envisaged. Some of this – our infamous stainless-steel wind-posts needed to vertically stiffen the building – were custom-fabricated and were missing from the original budget as at that time they weren't mandatory. Overall though, this part of the budgeting was within 10% of forecast.

We were way off on the fit-out costs. There were some omissions (we must have spent a couple of grand on nails, screws, and other fixings for example), and some changes (the oak staircase for example) but generally the price of materials had increased significantly between forming the original budget and actually starting to build. There were also some under-estimations in quantities. For example, that staple of the building industry – four-by-two timber: we used about ten times what we'd originally estimated and for a period seldom a day went by without another delivery of it turning up. And I lost count of the number of skip-loads of construction debris which were collected.

We also had some unexpected costs. I've mentioned already the substantially larger legal and professional fees as a result of wrangling over the lease. The additional steelwork added thousands of pounds. We had to hire a site office and toilets for much longer than expected, and installation of some of the utilities involved more groundworks than we had envisaged. There wasn't much we could do about any of them except swallow them and carry on.

With hindsight we could have continually reviewed and revised the budget during the fund-raising period, but this wouldn't have actually changed anything. Indeed, it could have made things worse since it would have pushed back the start of construction whilst we raised more money, and material costs could have increased further in this time. Likewise, we could have stopped at the point the bank account was empty. But at that stage the building was 90% complete but still unusable, so we took the view that we would press on and borrow what was needed to finish. Not ideal since the Group ended the project with a debt which was one of the things we wanted to avoid, but really there was no attractive alternative.

A DIY build

We could have adopted the conventional method to construct our hall. We could have engaged an architect to draw up the plans, and used a main contractor to be responsible for the actual construction. This was the route assumed by the Parish's professional advisers when telling us our budget was one-quarter of that which would actually be needed. There is some value in using a tried-and-tested method since it removes a lot of the uncertainty around timescales. It assigns responsibility for the project completion, ensures everyone is building against a complete set of plans, avoids resource shortfalls, and provides contingency against the unexpected. It also comes at a high price which we knew we couldn't afford. Going back to the inception of the project in 2012, had we stood up in front of the parents and said we have this great idea to build our own Scout Hall but that it will cost £¾ million and we'd like them to raise that amount then the project would have died there and then. We knew there was only one approach which would work: to manage the project ourselves and to construct it à la Grand Designs very much as a DIY build.

We knew that although this would be the most cost-effective build approach, it would not be the quickest. However, a fast build wasn't a priority; we were under no pressure to vacate our temporary meeting place at our host Scout Group and our temporary equipment storage at Redhill Aerodrome was both secure and reasonably long term. Within reason, building it could take the time it needed.

What this approach would give us was:

- Full control over what was built: designed and constructed to meet our own requirements
- A great sense of ownership by everyone physically involved in any element of the construction or finishing
- A focal point to bring the Group together and have a laugh or two.

Throughout the build phase we had available what became known as Scout TV. In essence this was a webcam strategically positioned to oversee the building site and anyone could access it from our website and watch the progress. This became sadly compulsive viewing for some of us, and was also a mechanism for wives to find out where their husbands were if they recognized cars parked on site. With Norwegian Air offering free Wi-Fi on their flights, there's a photo of me viewing Scout TV at 35,000 feet on route to Copenhagen. I said it was sadly compulsive.

Although we managed the project ourselves there were certain tasks we could undertake and those which we needed to sub out. The next couple of sections explain these in more detail.

What we could not do ourselves

The construction of the water-tight building shell was largely subbed out against fixed-price work-packages. This was mostly the reason this phase of the project a) came in on time and b) pretty much held up against the budget. We sub-contracted:

- The demolition and site clearance (even though some of us were itching to break out the sledgehammers)
- The groundworks for the new foundations and utilities
- Construction to roof-plate level (labour only; David estimated and ordered the number of bricks required and without exaggeration we

ended up with three whole bricks left over at the end. Just as well since they were on a 40-week lead-time to resupply.)

- Roof trusses and ply boarding (again labour only, the ply boarding came from our reclaimed site hoardings)
- Supply and installation of the zinc roof to match the Parish Centre
- Installation of the fascias, soffits, guttering (though we installed the downpipes ourselves)
- Supply and installation of the windows and doors
- First and second fix electrical and mechanical
- Supply and installation of the disabled lift
- Plastering and the trickier bits of dry-lining
- Door-hanging (internal; we fitted the roller shutters and garage doors ourselves)
- Fitting carpets and vinyl floor coverings

The UK building industry often comes in for a lot of stick both in the Press and generally: expensive, poor quality, lazy, on permanent tea-breaks and so on. Speak to most people who have used builders and often somewhere in the conversation will be horror stories: gripes about what went wrong, what their builder did or didn't do. For our project, the opposite was true. Without exception we had the best sub-contractors we could have hoped for. They came to us mainly via Paul, our construction-company dad who also offered his services gratis as construction manager. He supplied us with a ready-made workforce who were genuinely interested in the project and often went the extra mile. In some respects, at times it became more DIY SOS that Grand Designs. Many of them came to the opening ceremony, not least so they could see the finished product and I think they were proud to have been part of it. Some of them too had a keen sense of humour. I enquired of one of our Irish chippies doing the roof whether they'd be working on Good Friday. Quick as anything he replied "No, no", pausing before continuing "not the best day to be hammering nails into a piece of wood by a Catholic church!"

What we could do ourselves

Now we get to the fun bit. With a few of us keen on DIY, we figured we could do much of the fit-out ourselves. This was a tad ambitious. The list of what we actually did accomplish ourselves is quite long and impressive, and included:

- Dry-lining ceilings (where we could reach them)
- Constructing stud walls
- Constructing false ceilings
- Insulating ceilings and floors
- Fitting skirting boards and architraves
- Any boxing-in required and construction of all cupboards and storage
- Installing the staircase
- All of the painting
- Tiling in washrooms and kitchen
- Internal glazing
- Fitting the oak flooring in the main hall
- Installing the climbing wall
- Installing the kitchen
- Internal plumbing and installation of washroom fittings
- Installation of the lightning conductors

> **An alternate way of looking at things**
>
> John: Mike, we have a problem...
>
> Me: No we don't
>
> John: Yes we do
>
> Me: No John, we have an opportunity to succeed.
>
> (A short while later)
>
> John: Mike, we have another opportunity to succeed...

All of this was accomplished by teams of volunteers. We would send out an email towards the end of each week to all of our parents explaining what was on the job-list for the following weekend, and asking for a couple of hours of their time. The time commitment grew; initially starting off as a few hours on a Saturday morning this became all day Saturday then all weekend, and in the month before we opened the building, pretty much every evening as well. As might be expected there was a hard-core of the same people who turned up regularly, but by the end I estimated that over 80% of the Group had been involved somewhere along the line. We were exceptionally fortunate to have one Explorer parent, a self-employed builder who put an enormous amount of support into the project. Also, unlike most of us he knew what he was doing. So when the oak staircase turned up on a van as a massive jigsaw puzzle with no instructions we looked at it, looked at him, said "Michael would you be able to…" and half a day later it was installed.

Occasionally help was sparse and we moaned about "always the same few down here…", especially over summer when many families were on holiday. But at the end of the day we clearly had the right amount of help as we opened the building on the day we said we would with a building finished bar the snagging.

It's worth highlighting four specifics from the above list of things we did ourselves in case anyone is foolish enough to attempt the same.

Stud walls

Technically, we sub-contracted the construction of some of the stud walls. For about two years we had been discussing the project with the local technical college, which was interested in using it to provide practical experience for its students taking vocational building courses: brick-laying, painting, carpentry and the like. David and I had been to the college to look at some of their coursework and had come away immensely impressed by the standard achieved. They were keen to be involved, we were keen to let them. It would be a great example of local young people supporting a community project to be used by other local young people.

In the end though the delayed start to construction mostly defeated the idea since the fit-out didn't start until April and the students' courses ended in June whereupon they would all disappear for the summer. The one thing which did work out time-wise was construction of many of the stud walls. We supplied the timber, the college supplied the supervised labour. And it was pretty successful. Allowed only hammers, nails, and handsaws (so no power-tools) an army of students descended for a few weeks and, with varying degrees of enthusiasm, got most of the stud walls up. The only thing which prevented them from completing were the health and safety elves. The site had not been properly risk-assessed and was eventually deemed too dangerous for students as we did not have a full-time foreman on site. Reluctantly for both the college and us, we had to call it quits. But they had helped to move us forward and we were very grateful. Later they constructed a pair of barn doors for the Parish store, which is a permanent display of their skill and cooperation.

The rest of the stud-walls we built ourselves. This gave the opportunity for some of us to buy new toys on the justification that "well it will be useful for DIY once this is done". A laser level was purchased, which made putting in vertical studs and horizontal dropped ceilings a doddle. A super-accurate compound mitre saw on a stand was acquired, so we could cut four-by-two and other timber accurately. And most popular, I bought a nail-gun! Firing 90mm nails this made completing the stud walls and other structural timberwork dead easy and once over the shock of the noise of it firing in the nails then all of the blokes, with dreams of being Rambo, wanted a go with it. We got through two boxes of nails – some 5,000 – and I reckon I put in less than a third of these.

Laying the oak flooring

I have described on page 54 how we had salvaged four tonnes of solid oak flooring and moved it six times to its final resting place in the new hall. Now it had to be laid again. We'd thought, rather over-optimistically, that if it had taken only a few hours to lift then it wouldn't take much more than a weekend to put it all back down again. It took the best part of three weeks. It took a weekend to lay the first metre, which we celebrated with a few beers whilst looking at the next seventeen metres to go. Each piece of oak had to be cut to length and tapped into position with a sledgehammer so the tongue and groove married together and fitted flush. Then it had to be nailed into position using a floor-nailer bought especially for the job. And thousands of nails were needed. If the nailer wasn't struck exactly right then the nail would sit proud in the groove in the plank, preventing the next plank from seating correctly. Injuries abounded – splinters from the oak, bruised shins from missing the timber whilst using the sledgehammer, and swollen thumbs from missing the anvil on the nailer. Various volunteers had a go at this, but in the end it was two grandfathers who got into a routine and worked tirelessly to get it all finished. The end result looks superb.

Insulating ceilings and floors

Without a doubt this was the grottiest job we had to do. All of the ceilings and in between the floor joists had to be filled with insulation. Mostly we used rolls of fibreglass as they were cheap but it was horrible stuff to work with. Cutting it into joist-widths released a cloud of fibreglass particles which settled on skin and hair like itching powder. It settled on the floor, raising clouds of fibres whenever anyone walked past. Starting off with dust-masks and gloves, the insulation-fitters rapidly progressed to full body suits on the basis it was better to sweat buckets in those than suffer the fibreglass. It wasn't even easy to install. Under the floor was bad enough as a mountain of materials had to be moved around all of the time to give access, and our plywood flooring which had been nail-gunned into place by the carpenters had to be pried up before the insulation could be laid. It was even worse installing it in the ceiling where the insulation-fitters were working atop a scaffold tower, laying it into the gaps and then having to staple strings across it to keep it in position before the dry-lining went up.

We realized we'd forgotten to insulate above one of the false ceilings and by this time most of the ceiling had been dry-lined ready for plastering. There was one small gap left so we poked one of our former Explorers, who is very tall and thin, through it and refused to let him come down until the job was done. Slave labour? Absolutely!

We sub-contracted the trickier ceiling dry-lining to a firm of Polish builders who later also did a fantastic job plastering where needed. The only snag was a massive language barrier – only one of them spoke English and he wasn't always there. We became adept at communicating using hand-signals and pencil diagrams and generally got by. We did learn though to get on site at weekends before them, to race to be first to turn on the radio. If we were too late then we ended up listening to a Polish station all day.

Painting

When we asked for help with many of the building jobs, we sometimes got a poor response because people felt they didn't know how to do what was needed – they were outside their comfort zone. Painting was different. Many people paint and decorate in their own homes so had experience. Lots of people thus felt they could help and we had so much support we had to buy additional brushes and rollers. The trouble was, we found, that there was sometimes a difference between ambition and aptitude. One parent turned up to help and was asked if he could paint some skirting and architrave. He was, he told us, quite good at painting. Well he certainly painted what we had asked, and also, with great enthusiasm, painted beyond the woodwork onto the freshly-emulsioned walls. And floor. And radiators. And the disabled lift. There was paint everywhere. When he said it was time for him to leave we didn't argue and someone then went round again with the emulsion brush and razor blade covering up or scraping off the excess.

Painting was one of the few activities we could get the kids involved with too. Some of them got quite enthusiastic and painted the same piece of wall over and over again. We did run the same risk as for car-washing – a paint-brush dropped onto the dusty floor would be picked up and continued to be used, introducing a textured effect to the wall which later had to be scraped back and discretely repainted when the helper had departed.

Our painters had a tendency simply to abandon both brush or roller and paint-tray when they left. After a couple of times walking in the next morning to discover rock-hard bristles and roller-sleeves, John took responsibility for taking everything home at the end of a day and cleaning them in his bath. He remains mute on whether he was in the bath at the same time, but we have our suspicions.

Painting was the one activity which really brought the Group together. Parents who felt they'd been unable to contribute before owing to a lack of skill or confidence got involved in the painting. Kids painted the walls. There was a tangible sense of the project drawing to a close. There was pride in their work and a sense of achievement. They could point to an area and say "I painted that" or (in the case of two of our regular cooks in the kitchen), "I tiled/grouted that". And there is justification in being proud; professional builders have looked at the standard of what we achieved and cannot believe it's been done by a bunch of amateurs.

> ### Leggetts
>
> One of our parents introduced a new noun into our site vocabulary. A Parishioner, a lovely gentleman whose surname is in no way the same as the title of this box, offered to help paint. He was quite enthusiastic with his brush-strokes and very often blobs of paint would be found some considerable distance from where he was working. Sometimes he would spot these and attempt to clean them off with his handkerchief, resulting in an even bigger mess as the paint smeared.
>
> A parent, whilst painting, was heard to say "oh no I've made a leggett" when he splodged paint onto the floor. Thus the noun was born.
>
> **leggett** *leg'et, n.* a splash of paint, often smeared, found at an infeasible distance from its source. Its origin may or may not be obvious depending on who is holding a paintbrush nearby.

There is no doubt that doing much of the work ourselves had a benefit to 17th Reigate which went way beyond merely financial. We got to know each other better. We found out about each other's jobs, families, hobbies. We learned what we each favoured in a packed lunch. We knew what food we were willing to share and which would receive a fork in the back of the hand if anyone tried to nick it. We learned off each other, some learning more than others. We understood areas of expertise and comfort-zones, and what we could really achieve when pushed. We shared humour, music, banter, and a common sense of purpose. We grew together as a Group. Throughout all of this we had a tremendous crew of friends and relatives providing support, either practically as part of the DIY team or keeping that team fed and watered with tea and biscuits. 17th Reigate will remain forever indebted to all who rolled up their sleeves, metaphorically or actually, and helped build something special.

The opening ceremony

Completing the build in the Group's centenary year was something special, and we wanted to mark the occasion appropriately with a formal opening and big party. We settled on a date (see box on the following page) and started the preparations early. We were making a massive assumption that the building would actually be completed by that date; it would not have looked good to have sent invitations out and then recalled them because we weren't ready. For a long time, readiness did indeed look shaky but as in so many building projects, a month before completion the site looks, well, a building site but then a miracle happens and everything gets done. This is pretty much what happened with us. As the date drew closer, weekend work became weekends and every evening and the volume of help from our volunteers rocketed. Our local hardware stores benefited as well. We were extremely fortunate in that two of the best-known chain-stores supplying screws and tools had recently opened branches five minutes away. These were frequented to the point we were on first-name terms with the counter staff and we could have saved time by permanently situating someone there taking telephone orders from the site.

Planning started around six months before the opening date, with a rough plan. We knew the priority was to send out invitations far and wide and get the date into people's diaries. We included local dignitaries, the Scouting community, anyone who had been involved in delivering the project or supporting us financially, friends, family, former Group members, and anyone else we could think of. We wanted a big celebration.

September 19th 2015

This was the date of the hall opening. Originally it had been agreed to be one week later, on 26th September, and we could have really done with the extra week to finish off.

I then remembered I had tickets for England vs. Wales in the Rugby World Cup on 26th. I did suggest the opening still went ahead on that date and that I would raise a celebratory pint of Guinness from the terraces at Twickenham at the hour of opening. However, my Executive Committee members were kind enough to agree that the date should be moved forward so I could attend, and midnight oil was burned accordingly.

In view of the match result, I would have been happier if the original opening date had been held and I'd gone to that instead.

The planning and execution cycle ran something like as follows:

T-6 months: Agree the opening date, start a rough plan of action for the day, plan the invitation list, start to compile mailing list, book Parish Centre (as overflow)

T-5 months: Change the opening date (see box above), re-book celebratory Mass, re-book Parish Centre

T-4 months: Print and post the invitations, track responses

T-2 months:	Send reminders to those who hadn't responded, firm up on the planning for the day, confirm who will be actually formally opening the building
T-1 month:	Confirm catering arrangements (parents to be asked to bring a plate of food to share). Wine purchased. Wine sampled. More wine purchased. Explorers coerced as either waiters or greeters for the dignitaries. Local and Scouting Press notified.
T-0 (the day):	Morning:

Panic with lots of last-minute jobs. Everywhere swept and vacuumed. Chairs set out, place-names stencilled (on John's orders) for reserved seating, audio-visual checked, running order rehearsed. Running order changed. Running order re-rehearsed. Running order changed back. Our youngest Beaver found and coached on breaking the flag. Contingency Beaver found as youngest decided he didn't want to break the flag. Youngest Beaver receives comforting words from his mum and is then okay to break flag. Step-ladder found so youngest Beaver could actually reach the flag.

Afternoon (final running order):

- Opening address (by our Chairman)
- How we got to here (by Group Scout Leader)
- Formal opening (by the Mayor)
- The first flag-break (by our youngest Beaver)
- Addresses from Scouting District and County
- Celebration Mass and Church Parade
- Formal blessing of the building (by the Bishop of Arundel and Brighton)

The actual day passed in a blur but was a huge success and we received endless compliments on what we had built. The Worshipful the Mayor of the Borough of Reigate and Banstead duly unveiled the opening plaque and gave us great praise in our accomplishment. She described us as an inspiration to others and stressed that when a group of community volunteers get together around a common purpose then they really can move mountains.

Of particular significance was the Blessing of the building by the Diocese of Arundel and Brighton's new Bishop. Bishop Richard is a great supporter of Scouting and is Episcopal Advisor to the National Catholic Scout Fellowship. He had been to see the new hall when it was still a building site so it was entirely fitting that we asked him to Bless the hall after our Celebration Mass.

What was really nice was the number of people who had turned out – we reckon we had easily three hundred present, way more than the chairs we had available so it was standing room only at the back. And it was great to see so many of our supporters there, many of those we'd only ever spoken to on the phone or via email. To be able to meet these face to face and thank them personally was something special and they got to see how their money had been spent.

In one of those weird coincidences, the date of our formal opening was the same as Fr. Chris's (our Parish Moderator and stalwart supporter of our Group) fiftieth birthday. So many of us ended one party and went across into the Parish Centre to join in another. It was a good day.

Finishing off and the snagging list

During the month after our formal opening we did nothing other than use the building as intended – for Section meetings. There was still a raft of odds and ends to finish off but after the frenetic dash to the finishing line there wasn't the appetite to immediately carry on. We did get together and compile a snagging list which ran to a couple of A4 pages, and we prioritized according to the importance of them and thus whether they ought to be resolved in the next month, three months, year and so on.

Which led to an interesting and unexpected reaction – when we published the snagging list and asked for help with some of the jobs, there was <u>still</u> no appetite to carry on! It seems that for many people who had helped in the run-up to opening the hall, opening the hall equated to the end of the project. We have gradually worked through the snagging list with the same core of volunteers but it has been much harder work than we were expecting.

The other interesting thing to emerge is that we have all had to go through a change of mind-set; from one focused on getting the hall built to now appreciating that the Group has an asset which needs to be managed, maintained, and its debt paid off. It took a while for this to sink in with all of us; this is the first time the Group has ever found itself in this position and it takes some getting used to. To ease this transition, we've changed part of the structure of the Executive Committee, from a sub-committee managing the <u>build</u> to one managing the <u>building</u>. A subtle distinction but an important one as it puts the responsibility for administering the asset where it needs to be.

For all intents and purposes the project is now finished. The next chapter in the life of 17th Reigate Scout Group has started, with the expectation of another fifty years of adventures, challenges, opportunities, and fun for the Group's young people. Now that really is a worthy legacy for future generations.

In conclusion, what did we learn?

Involve the users in the design process

From early on we sought opinions from those who would be using the hall the most – our Leaders and young people – on what they would like to see included in the design. The serving hatch between hall and kitchen, the climbing wall, storage layout, and building security either came directly from these discussions or were influenced by them. We would have failed, we thought, if we produced a facility where practicalities had been ignored or not considered.

It won't all be plain sailing

Very few building projects ever run exactly to plan or budget. There are usually factors outside immediate control which will blow the project off course. In our case we had to contend with poor weather, global materials shortages, and a booming building industry which sucked up resources and extended lead-times. Fortunately, we had no hard deadline by when we needed to be finished (there was a hard-stop completion date in the lease but that was changed) but that won't necessarily always be the case.

"Keep your friends close and your enemies closer"

"The Art of War", Sun-Tzu (Chinese general & military strategist ~400 BC)

OK so we weren't exactly engaged in warfare but we were surprised to discover that some of our original supporters proved less-keen on the idea at the point we said we were ready to start building. Nimby-ism[6], not invented here, resistance to change... we never really understood why we were getting such a hard time and to be honest, we didn't care. We had righteousness on our side, we felt! Through a combination of tact, diplomacy, passion for the cause, and "well we're doing it anyway" (the most effective) we won through and construction could start.

Round pegs into square holes

We got a much better response to our pleas for weekly help when volunteers actually knew what was needed to complete the task and they felt comfortable in what they were doing. Interestingly despite being a cornerstone of Scouting, the "I've never done it before but I'll give it a go" attitude was seldom seen.

---

[6] Not in my back yard

We did find that we could build skills and confidence gently. Most volunteers, for example, had never dry-lined a ceiling with plasterboard. So the first few attempts were done with an army of people supporting both physically and morally, offering advice (helpful or not) and refining the technique until a much smaller team had the skill to carry on and complete.

Celebrate success (even the small wins)

During any one weekend there was around 10%-15% of total volunteers available actually on site. It was important, therefore, that we regularly told the other 85%-90% what had been accomplished and what was on the list for the following week. In this weekly email we also thanked by name all of those who had given up their time the previous weekend.

Get the kids involved

From the outset we wanted the young people involved where they could in the actual construction. Obviously building sites are inherently dangerous places which severely limited the options on what they could do and when, but tasks such as painting walls were prime candidates.

We also realized that if kids were down assisting then we would most likely also have their mums and dads!

Invite the world

Formally opening a project such as this one is a big deal and deserves to be marked in style. Many people – in our case hundreds – had been involved in the project at various stages and all needed to be thanked and for them to be able to see the fruits of their labour (or money). At a point in the project when funds were not only low but severely in the red, there was discussion on whether the Group could afford a big party. We took the hit – the benefits of inviting the world to see what we had achieved were overwhelmingly compelling.

Humour is king, but be prepared for grumpiness

There is no doubt that people worked much better and were more willing to come along and help if they thought it would be good fun, and they'd have a few laughs. I don't mean that a site comedian is a pre-requisite (though we did have a few of these) but greeting people with a smile and gentle banter throughout the day undoubtedly helped the team spirit.

It couldn't be like that all of the time – as the opening day drew closer then on occasions tensions and grumpiness did increase but never to the point of blazing rows and usually there was enough humour elsewhere to counter whoever had the hump. Gritted teeth were required, though, when faced with acres of bare plastered walls, a volunteer would arrive on site and ask "so what needs painting?".

It's not over when it's over

The army of volunteers who had worked evenings and weekends on top of full-time jobs to complete the hall collectively breathed a sigh of relief at the end of the opening ceremony... well, it was finished, wasn't it? They looked forward, not unreasonably, to getting their lives back.

But building projects seldom, if ever, completely end – there is always something to do, whether snagging, maintenance, replacing failed fittings, or whatever. In our case there was a long snagging list and it proved very difficult to motivate people to carry on, to give up even more of their time, once the hall was up and running.

Embrace the future

Once the building was opened, largely finished, and in use the reality dawned that processes and procedures needed to be put in place to run it and to manage it as an asset. This required a different mind-set and skillset – akin to moving a business from a start-up phase into establishment and growth. It took several months for us to appreciate this and collectively get our heads around it, but it is an important requirement and should not be overlooked.

Postscript

This has been written some six months after the formal opening. During that time, we have seen growth in the Group – we have opened a second Beaver Colony as promised, led by a marvellous group of brand-new Leaders who stepped forward to run it. In twelve months' time we expect to open a second Cub Pack and later, additional Scout and Explorer units. Our waiting lists remain undiminished; I was expecting the Beaver waiting list to reduce after we opened the second Colony but all that happened was more parents added the names of their children. We now have at least a sixteen-year "supply" of young people to go through the Group. More adults have stepped forward to help too, not just to run our new Beaver Colony but across most of the other Sections as well. Long may this honeymoon period continue.

We've been able to expand the range of activities on offer. Tony's inspirational climbing wall is proving immensely popular and helps to develop a child's confidence in a safe environment. We've added air-rifle shooting for the Scouts and Explorers, and indoor archery available across the Group. Our Explorers took part in their first-ever online jamboree, reaching other Scout Groups across the globe and sharing stories internationally. Our Beaver and Cub Sections held their first-ever sleepovers in the hall, with great success and excitement (but not much sleep). Most recently the 17th Reigate flying club has started, using the hall as a venue for flying model helicopters and drones. Boys and their toys.

The hall is catering to other community groups too as we promised it would. Without any advertising we get routine bookings ranging from mother and toddler groups, Co-workers of Mother Teresa, a Guide group, District Scouting meetings and others. The hall has been used on multiple occasions for children's birthday parties and we have even hosted an international Bridge tournament. Evenings remain sacrosanct though – we built the hall for our Scout Group and will not compromise the times when we want it available.

At this stage there are still some unknowns. What will the building really cost to run over the course of a year, and what will be the impact of this on our fund-raising? How well will the building stand up to the rigours of use by energetic young people five nights out of seven? Long-term how does the building measure up against some of its design goals – security and building operation for example. We're a way off from knowing the answers but the early signs are good and we have the structure and stability to deal with the answers (and more opportunities to succeed) in due course.

But as of today without a shadow of doubt the project has exceeded expectations and provided our young people with a facility which is the envy of many and of which they (and we) can be proud. My closing words to them in my speech at the opening ceremony still resonate: "what you get out of it *(the building)* is down to you, but have fun in it – that's what it's been built for".

Bibliography

Burnett, Ken (2006). *The Zen of Fundraising.* Jossey-Bass

Whaley, Simon (2007). *Fundraising for a Community Project.* Howtobooks

Farnhill, Jonathan (2007). *The Porcupine Principle and other fundraising secrets.* Directory of Social Change

Wheildon, Colin (ed) (2005). *Type & Layout. Are you communicating or just making pretty shapes.* The Worsley Press

Botting Herbst, Nina & Norton, Michael (ed) (2012). *The Complete Fundraising Handbook.* Directory of Social Change

Eastwood, Mike & Norton, Michael (ed) (2010) *Writing Better Fundraising Applications: A Practical Guide.* Directory of Social Change

Wheildon, Colin (ed) (1996) *Type and Layout: How Typography and Design Can Get Your Message Across - Or get in the Way.* Strathmore Press

Funding Central database: www.fundingcentral.org.uk

Our website www.17threigate.org also contains information about our Group and the new hall, including a complete list of all organizations who offered us direct or indirect financial support.